The *Greenhorns*

–A WHIMSICAL TREATISE OF THEIR PERSUASIONS

BY

CHAS. S. ELINSKY

First published by AuthorHouse 12/13/04

ISBN: 1-4208-1703-5 (e)
ISBN: 1-4208-1702-7 (sc)

Library of Congress Control Number: 2004195082

Printed in the United States of America
Bloomington, Indiana

This book is printed on acid-free paper.

authorHOUSE

1663 LIBERTY DRIVE, SUITE 200
BLOOMINGTON, INDIANA 47403
(800) 839-8640
www.authorhouse.com

THIS BOOK IS DEDICATED TO MY PARENTS,
HARRY AND SARAH, OF BLESSED MEMORY.
THEY WERE TWO OF THE MOST LOVING
"GREENHORNS" EVER TO GRACE AMERICA.

....

I WISH TO EXPRESS GRATITUDE TO ANITA
SINGER WHOSE AFFECTION LED ME TO
BELIEVE IN MYSELF AGAIN.

....

A special thanks to Rabbi Stanley J.
Schachter who offered positive sug-
gestions for this book. From his
knowledge, I have learned; from his
wisdom, I have been inspired; from
his witticisms, I have laughed.

....

GRAPHIC DESIGN BY JEFF GREENE
WWW.JGREENE327@AOL.COM

ILLUSTRATIONS BY ALAN GOULDER
AND JOHN BEUKEMANN

CONTENTS

INTRODUCTION

The *Greenborns*

-A WHIMSICAL TREATISE OF THEIR PERSUASIONS

P lease indulge me through this first paragraph, as I need to make a point. I am tethered to an oxygen tube for lung disease. In addition, I suffer other problems that include: heart bypass, prostate cancer and hearing loss.

The above is absolutely true. Each night, I gather the new prosthetic parts provided by my surgeons (G-d's proto types apparently having malfunctioned) and carefully position them in a dresser drawer. The following morning, I attempt to reassemble the various components of my anatomical puzzle. If successful, I proceed to daily chores and limited pleasures. If I cannot put the pieces together, I think to myself "the hell with it;" return to bed and endeavor to try again the following day.

Do my problems compel you to smile or even laugh? Sure they do!

Why so? There are a couple of reasons. One, you feel relieved that you, the reader, have been spared similar indispositions and two; there have been mornings when you couldn't compose yourself so you empathize with me. Your debilities are in the past so you're joyful. Wittingly or unwittingly, you are displaying a Jewish characteristic not to dwell upon despair but to chuckle at the memory of it for humor helps to mask the pain. Jews, who have existed on a *cul-de-sac of misery* from the beginning of recorded time, due to debasement and degradation, have partially resorted to laughter to overcome the injustices.

Availing themselves of the whimsical, they have converted acerbic negatives into acceptable jocular positives that make them feel fit and proper. That, at the risk of over-simplification, is the essence of Jewish humor.

It is highly paradoxical that Jews accept redirecting misfortune into a benefit. But consider this: if tzorus (troubles) were eliminated, what would Jews talk about?

There are, of course, other contributing aspects in defining Jewish humor that hopefully will be determined as we examine one microscopic era of Jewish history, that of the Greenhorns.

PART ONE

✡ ✡ ✡ ✡ ✡ ✡ ✡ ✡ ✡ ✡ ✡ ✡

Not the power to remember, but its very opposite, the power to forget, is a necessary condition of our existence.

--Sholem Asch

Jewish Greenhorns (newly arrived immigrants to America during the mass immigration era of 1880 to 1940) formed a cornucopia of levity and humor that continues to exist. The Greenhorns' influences proliferated many discussions relative to the genesis, value and benefit of Jewish humor.

It is noted that the term "*Greenhorns*" was widely used by American citizens to describe the immigrants who frequently utilized the term themselves as indictable against inadequacy or failure. Examples:

"My tie doesn't match the suit. That's what Greenhorns wore in Europe." "My greena cousina (cousin-feminine) don't speak so good Ainglish but she's a good matzah ball soup maker." Etc., etc.

There were some immigrants, anxious to be accepted into the American society, who considered the term "Greenhorns" offensive and derogatory but the usage so permeated their lives that most learned to ignore the term. The label became somewhat obsolete and therefore, rarely applied to current immigrants. However, it is important to remember the Greenhorn era as a significant part of Jewish history.

All of our people all over the country–except pure blooded indians, are immigrants or the descendants of immigrants, including even those that came over on the Mayflower.

--Franklin Delano Roosevelt

We Jews seem to perceive what makes us jovial, but we have failed to put the rationale into written words that others can understand. This essay is a modest attempt to remedy that omission and to display the Jewish immigrants' persuasions and influences in America together with some of the humorous experiences that emanated from that era. It is noted that the Greenhorns made enormous contributions to the United States but not without suffering adversity. They sailed on the Atlantic sea only to encounter a new sea, "sea of troubles," to use a Shakespearean term. (No. Willie was not Jewish).

Greenhorns were confronted with perplexities brought on by residing in a new country and adopting a new language that they found awkward and complicated. Their effort to assimilate despite reluctant acceptance was arduous. In addition, the newcomers' efforts to learn and acquire new customs led to ridicule and conversely, to a few sympathetic smiles.

The dictionary differentiates between immigration, (the act of coming to a foreign country to live) and emigration (the act of fleeing because of political persecution). For the purpose of this text, all immigrants are referred to as Greenhorns. "There were, of course, millions of Greenhorns other than Jews but their odysseys are not for me to undertake. Immigrants were often erroneously labeled refugees and after World War ll, displaced persons. It is estimated that about 15% of all immigrants have returned to their respective lands. It is to the benefit of the United States to have graciously given residence to another country's brain drain

Introduced to a new linguistic environment, the Greenhorns found it extremely difficult to learn English, a language of many oxymora such as civil war, original copy and student teacher. English is a language that is also comprised of multiple homonyms that obstruct the pathway to learning.

Teachers taxed the minds of immigrants by introducing words such as bore-boar, seen-scene, tail-tale and suite-sweet. Then they changed the infinitive almost totally: teach-taught but not preach- praught; slay-slew but not play-plew. Try to convince an Orthodox Jew there is no ham in kosher hamburger, that sweetmeats are just candies, heart of artichoke is a vegetable, and that a Guinea pig is not a pig. There were sufficient complexities to have made an immigrant almost return to his homeland!

Yiddish bears the marks of our expulsions from land to land, the language which absorbed the laments of generations, the poison and the bitterness of history, the language whose precious jewels are undried, uncongealed Jewish tears.

--I.L. Peretz

Although from various countries, the Jewish Greenhorns brought with them a common language, Yiddish, which is a fusion of several languages with German as its base. It uses Hebrew letters, arthritic cadence with expressive hands and body English to establish a point..

Yankel Levine was lost in New York. He approached a friendly- looking man wearing a skullcap and asked if he could direct him to Delancy Street.

"Hold these packages," Yankel was told. After he complied, the man lifted his arms to his waistline with palms upward; shrugged his shoulders and asked, "How should I know?"

In a thousand years, Yiddish had become the natural language of ordinary European Jewry. There is a consensus among linguists that its origin was in the Rhine Valley, assembled with components from Jews migrating from the Mediterranean area and the Slovakian countries. Yiddish is similar to German with added words and expressions from Eastern Europe. One can find words in Polish, Russian, Hebrew, Lithuanian and others in its conformation.

Jewish expressions, aphorisms, and proverbs used by the Greenhorns are descriptive and psychologically stimulating. Jewish immigrant mothers scolded misbehaving children by expressing fondness, "You should have children just as bad as you are" or "A health on your navel." Some responses to questions were intended to be evasive by responding to a question with a question. When a customer asked a proprietor, "How's business?" the response was standard, "How should it be?"

Yiddish expressions did not always translate literally as intended. For example, "Keep quiet and eat," translated into a literal English pronouncement such as "Shut your mouth and eat!" Or this one; "Pay attention to your back" became " Give a look at your back."

Goldie was pulled out of the water while an excited crowd repeatedly yelled, "Get her husband; get her husband!"

"Stand back and give her air," commanded the lifeguard. "I'm going to give her artificial respiration." "No, you don't," yelled Bernie, her husband. "To my Goldie, you give real respiration."

A number of Yiddish words were adopted into the English language due to frequency of usage by gentiles as well as Jews. The following Yiddish words were selected at random as examples and can be found in most English dictionaries.

1)	Bagel	donut shaped roll
2)	Chutzpah	audacity, nerve
3)	Gelt	money
4)	Kosher	ok or fit for consumption
5)	Mish mash	hodge podge

6)	Maven	expert
7)	Schlep	drag
8)	Schmo	dolt
9)	Shamas	sexton, detective
10)	Tush	buttocks

In Yiddish, comparatives and superlatives do not always perform grammatically. Ask a Greenhorn, " How does one say in Yiddish," 'rich, richer, richest?'" You'll receive the likely answer, " a little money, in good shape and over-stuffed."

"Die cow hat uber die moon gejumped" is not Yiddish.

A customer called Mendel, the proprietor of a kosher restaurant, to his table to compliment him on how well the new Chinese waiter was learning Yiddish. "Sh," cautioned Mendel, "He thinks we're teaching him English."

It saddens me to write that Yiddish is a declining language due to linguistic assimilation and the predominant languages of English, French, Russian and Spanish being utilized. The world of communication has become much smaller and quicker than it was one hundred years ago so that the necessity for an interlacing language is no longer required. There are efforts to save Yiddish and its etymology, but the endeavors are in a primary state with some cultural attempts to reinstate it for the purpose of preserving its wonderful literature and descriptive expressions. There are several active organizations for the revival of

Yiddish: the National Yiddish Book Center of Amherst, Maine, the Yivo Institute for Jewish Research, the Hebrew University of Jerusalem and Workman's Circle just to name a few.

Immigration is the sincerest form of flattery.
--Jack Paar

PART TWO

I am free of prejudices. I hate everyone equally.

--W.C. Fields

Anti-Semitism, non-acceptance, or ostensibly the embarrassment from foreign characteristics, induced many Jewish newcomers and/or their progeny to Anglicize their names. The reasons for a myriad number of names being shortened or altered vary but the phenomenon probably occurred mostly due to the ideological theory of assimilation. Some simply changed their names for expediency and cosmopolitan flexibility. This was particularly true of movie actors and producers.

Famous among these were: Woody Allen, formerly Allan Konigsberg, Jack Benny (Benjamin Kubelsky), Milton Berle (Berlinger), Kirk Douglas (Isadore Demsky), and Walter Matthau (Matuschanskavasky). Max Anderson, the first Jewish film producer was born Max Aronson.

If my name were Lipschitz, I'd change it, too.

There were several eminent movie directors that came to America from Europe. Ernest Lubitsch, Erich von Stroheim, William Wyler and Billy Wilder to name just a few.

Billy Wilder, the most famous, was born in Austria in 1906 and later moved to Berlin, Germany. He emigrated from Germany's Nazi regime bringing his talent and skills to the United States where he became a citizen. He found his way to Hollywood where he eventually became a screenwriter and an award-winning director. His specialty was satirical plays.

Common among these esteemed persons was their wanderlust psyche. Most strayed from home at an early age. When one was asked if his parents objected, he said, "Are you kidding? They couldn't wait to rent out the room!"

There have been famous converts to Judaism; the most notable is probably Elizabeth Taylor who adopted the Hebrew name, Elisheva Rachel. I wonder if she would consider introducing a promotion for a perfume under an OU (kosher seal) label. She could call it the *"Oil of Oi Veh."* It would go over big in Israel.

Anne Meara, comedy partner and wife of Jerry Stiller, is another Jewish convert. It is said she observes all Jewish holidays but reserves the right to enjoy wearing the color green on St. Patrick's Day while participating in the tandem festivities.

It has been reported that the Immigration Service doles out green cards to temporary citizens every weekday, unless it falls on St. Patrick's Day. Then the color green is locked away so the staff can watch the big parade.

Joseph Greenberg called his mother to announce his forthcoming marriage to a shiksha (non–Jewish girl).

"She's a wonderful person of Irish descent," he told her, "and will make a wonderful wife. I tried to get her to convert but she wouldn't do it, being an ardent Catholic. The only problem we're facing is finding a place to live."

"Nothing to worry about." he was told, "You can have my first floor bedroom, I'll move up to the third floor attic where I can throw myself out of the window!"

George Gershwin, famous composer, was born in Brooklyn of Russian Greenhorn parents and at the age of 21 wrote his biggest hit "Swanee" sung by another Jewish celebrity, Al Jolson, in The Jazz Singer. Most of the famous motion picture companies were founded by Jews. Included among these are Adolph Zukor, Daniel Frohman, Sam,Jack Albert and Harry Warner, Hal Roach and a host of others.

Izzy Leibovitz appeared in front of Judge Larry Birnbaum. "Your oner, I vant to change my name from Izzy Leibovitz to Frederick Smith." "That does not present a problem," stated Judge Birnbaum. "Just pay the court charges and your wish will be fulfilled."

Six months later, the new Frederick Smith reappeared in front of Judge Birnbaum and announced that he wished to change his name from Frederick Smith to Joseph Jones. "I recognize you, sir," he was told. "Weren't you in front of my bench a few months back; had your name changed from Leibovitz?" "Yes, your oner, but I vant to change it again cause ven I tell people my name, Frederick Smith, they always ask, 'Vat vas it before?'"

Modernizing Greenhorn names did not necessarily reflect abandonment of religion. As the men had been consecrated through circumcision into Israel, it would difficult to reattach severed fragments!

Freedom is the oxygen of the soul.

--Moshe Dayon

Ellis Island, the immigration station, handled a flow of approximately 15 million immigrants prior to its closing in 1954. Uniformed guards processed the immigrants who misconstrued the regimentation officials in comparing them to the oppressive military in the old country. The new arrivals were reluctant and/or too frightened to volunteer information and accepted without argument any statements or labeling by these uniformed officers and sentries. Their emotional vulnerability was easily penetrated and xenophobia was rampant for several years before the new settlers could feel somewhat at ease.

The fear of uniforms was so ingrained in these émigrés that very few allowed their sons or daughters to join the Boy or Girl Scouts of America. They surmised that these were junior military organizations.

Chaim Levy was admitted to the United States, entering the country through Ellis Island and residing in Brooklyn. He attended his first religious service at a Shul (Synagogue) in his adopted country, introduced himself to the Shamus,(sexton) as Shawn Ferguesson. The Shamus repeated the name in disbelieve. "Shawn Ferguesson, sounds Irish; what kind of Jewish name is that?"

"I'll tell you," said the newcomer, "My real name is Chaim Levy. When the guard in Ellis Island asked me my name, I was so scared, I couldn't remember; so I said, 'Schoyn fargessen.'" In Yiddish, that, of course, means, "already forgotten." The guard, assuming that was my real name, wrote Shawn Ferguesson on the official papers, so I let it be!"

The venerated Statue of Liberty in the New York Harbor above Liberty Island displays a plaque with a sonnet, " The

New Collossus," written by a Jew, Emma Lazarus.

She was inspired to write poetry protesting the persecution of the Jews in Russia. The most quoted lines of the sonnet are "Give me your tired, your poor, your huddled masses yearning to breathe free."

Biblical poem: Fleas – Adam Hadam

It is noted that Ellis Island was not the only port of entry for the Greenhorns. Castle Garden, on a small island off the Battery, was another immigration port, used from 1855 until 1890. It was closed due to filthy sanitation conditions.

Jews substituted the name and pronounced it "Kesselgarten" to describe a filthy cluttered area. Immigrant parents, mindful of the psychological transference, often dubbed their offsprings' bedrooms "Kesselgartens" demanding the areas be improved and enhanced. Greenhorn mothers were meteorologists They would walk into the kids' bedrooms and shout, "It looks like a hurricane went through your room." *And for certain you never heard a Jewish Greenhorn mother say, " Your cluttered room is a sign of creativity.* They would then dispatch their kids to their respective bedrooms until the rooms were reasonably presentable

The straightening task was fairly simple, for the area was limited to a bed, chair, dresser and, if lucky, a mirror. Today, parents, intending to ground for misbehaving, direct their kids to bedrooms that have a telephone, television, radio, computer, etc.

PART THREE

Superstition is the religion of feeble minds

--Edmond Burke

The Greenhorns did not believe in magic because it has long been considered an abomination. Despite the prohibition against divination, soothsaying, witchcraft or ghosts (Deuteronomy XV111-11), many of the Greenhorns brought superstitions and gullibility with them.

Although rabbis condemned superstitious practices, manifestations against self -created forces of potential evil did exist with the immigrants.

Many superstitions can be traced back to Egyptian times when the Jews were slaves and nurtured through Jewish mysticism. Jews are admonished in the Torah to avoid seers, wizards and false prophets.

Bert Stein approached a Wizard and inquired as to his ability to remove a curse. "Of course," responded the Wizard, "That is what I do best."

"I've had this curse for twenty years and I need you to rid me of it," Stein told him.

"State the exact words of the curse," cautioned Wizard.

"I now pronounce you man and wife."

Superstitious beliefs occur most often during times of stress or crisis. The most common to the Greenhorns was the power of a strange appearance or stare referred to as The Evil Eye. They were certain that the Evil Eye would bewitch and evoke evil spirits and demons. To insulate one's self from the Evil Eye, the Jews would utter the words, "No Evil Eye," and/or spit three times on the subject being threatened or in lieu of spitting, exclaim "Poo, Poo, Poo."

Spitting was believed to exert an insulating charm against witchcraft and was considered an antidote against the Evil Eye and witchcraft in general. Although the power of the spittle is mentioned several times in the New Testament and not in the Old Testament, many Jewish immigrants persisted in resorting to its powers.

Considering the number thirteen as unlucky was commonly based on thirteen people being present at the Last Supper. The fear of the number is so common, Webster's dictionary awarded it a name, "triskaidekaphobia." The number became a Christian omen for evil, misfortune and even death and therefore was not adopted by Jewish immigrants. Nor did they believe in wearing a rabbit's foot for good luck as the mistreatment of animals is forbidden in the Old Testament. *The logical thought was "If the rabbit's foot is lucky, why isn't it still with the rabbit?"* The Orthodox do not knock on wood, as it is considered a false and deceptive heathen practice apparently stemming from touching Christ's cross to ward off evil.

Many of the immigrants relied on the power of a red ribbon to repulse the threat of an evil omen. Immigrant mothers tied red ribbons to baby cribs and buggies in a continuous effort to drive away any harmful threats. The genesis of the practice has been lost in antiquity.

Walking under a ladder is another superstition that did not concern the immigrants.. It stemmed from an old Christian credo of the Holy Trinity. The Christians believed that to walk under a ladder was to intrude on sanctified areas because of the three sides formed.

Following the drinking of sacramental wine in a Jewish wedding rite, the shared glass by a bride and groom is put on the floor, where the groom tramples on and breaks it. The most common interpretation of this ritual is to remind one of the Temple destruction. *Most married men will tell you that the rite was the last time they were able to put their foot down.*

The Greenhorns did not put much credence into astrology, in which stars and planets influence terrestrial events. They did believe in fatalism (bashert) contingent upon their prayers and acts of kindness. The prophets chastised those that did believe in the heavenly bodies.(Is.7:13 and Jer.10.2.) The Talmud does contain several stories about astrologers interpreting correctly, but Maimonides considered it idolatry. His rabbinical disciples taught that Judaism was superior to stellar influence causing astrology to lose many Jewish proponents.

When a Jew sneezes, the common reaction is to wish one gezundeit (health). It probably originated with the belief that the heart stops beating during the severe action of a sneeze. Another common response has been, "G-d bless you!" Some immigrants believed the soul left the body for the moment. What does one say when G-d sneezes?

A mezuzah is a parchment piece from the hide of a kosher animal, with sacred scroll written by a sofer (scribe) in a container of various materials. It is affixed to the right side of one's doorpost required in most rooms owned by Jews. The injunction to do so appears in Deuteronomy 6:4-9 and 11:13-21. The Hebrew word "Shaddai" (Almighty) is on the back of the parchment and often on the container as well. As the parchment portion is hand inscribed, not machine printed, the mezuzah is costly.

The placement of the mezuzah was one of the most observed Greenhorns' commandments.

In addition to the commandment, they looked upon the mezuzah as a good luck charm, and it became fashionable to wear one to ward off evil spirits, despite the warning of Maimonides not to turn the words of G-d into an amulet. He instructed that the study of Torah produces immunity against evil. Some wore cloves of garlic in addition to the mezuza to ward off demons by their strong odor.

Mt. Sinai Hospital trustees voted to affix a mezuzah to each of the 500 patients' rooms. The trustee in charge of the program explained the procedure to the gentile maintenance man. He told him that the mezuzah was to be placed on the upper third of the doorpost to the right side with a slant towards the room. The maintenance man assured him that he would follow the procedure exactly.

After a week, the trustee was approached and told that all 500 mezuzahs were positioned properly as instructed. "Mr. Ginsburg," added the maintenance man, "to save you time and effort I removed and threw away all of the guarantees I found inside all of the mezuzahs.

Due mostly to language dissimilarities, many immigrants were given names substantially different than their original ones by custom officials. It was quite common for brothers to be provided with varied family names or ones with different spellings due to a calloused guard's indifference to accuracy. Some newcomers had names bestowed upon them according to their trade, craft, occupation or even disposition when an inspector could not discern his charge's name statement.

Examples:

CRAMER	A peddler who crammed a backpack
FROELICH	German derivative meaning joyful.
EBERMAN	Yiddish form for Abraham
NUSSBAUM	Nut tree
SCHNEIDER	Yiddish for tailor
BAUER	Farmer
SHEPHERD	Shepard
LEVY	A biblical terror - escort
GERSON	(Gersom) Hebrew from Gair stranger
GREENE	Complexion following 2 weeks on the seas
GOTTLIEB	German/Yiddish - Love God
SCHWARTZ	Black
WEISS	White
COHEN	Priest
ELINSKY	My own name. Nearest I can come - Ligner-Liar

Ashkenazic Jews name offspring after a deceased, holiday or event. In order to declare that the religion did not perish with the death of a loved one, a newborn may be identified with the same Hebrew name. They believe that the name is synonymous with the "neshuma" (soul) of the departed. Because it is common to name a baby after a deceased, one of the curses used upon an adversary was to utter, "You should have a baby named after you."

They also believe that one's life will be shortened if a baby were named after them. Conversely, the Sephardics from Spain, Portugal, North Africa, and Italy do not share this fear and one can find living parents and grandparents with the same names as their offspring. However, it is rare indeed to find Jewish names with a Junior or a Roman numeral tacked on. Moishe Jr. or Moishe the third is totally inconspicuous.

(Moishe) Moses was one of the most popular names for boys, given by Jewish immigrant parents hopeful that the newborn would follow in the prophet's righteous footsteps. *For those that know their bible, this is not understood, as they should recall that Moses was a basket case!* His namesakes are considered lucky that the Prince of Egypt wasn't called Nebuchadnezzar (king of Babylonia) or some such moniker. Esther was the most common name for a girl; given by Jewish parents in the hope that their daughter would reflect the beauty and spirit of the Purim Queen.

Because most births were not officially recorded in European countries, many Greenhorns did not know their exact birthdays. They were frequently given Hebrew names after heroes, heroines associated with the nearest Jewish holiday. My mother wanted to name me "Nuss" (nuts) after a Purim delicacy but was dissuaded by my sisters.

Virtuous expectations in the namesake's future were also

utilized for typical selections. Common choices were Mahir (swift, rapid), Nachum (comfort), Meir (one who brightens) and Zadik (righteous one). In addition, the parents paired or substituted the Hebrew names with common English ones to avoid possible embarrassment. It is interesting to note, that due to the passion for Israel, there is a trend reversal to using biblical names only again today.

Two women met on the street. "What an adorable baby," said one, "what's his name?"

"Schmuel" came the response. "We named him after his grandfather, Steve."

The main Jewish immigration to the United States occurred in the late 1800s and the early 1900s just prior to the Great Depression. It is estimated that only 250,000 Jews lived in the United States in 1880, but the next 50 years saw three million reach these shores. This mass influx was apparently caused by the persecution in Eastern Europe and the pogroms that started in 1881. Thousands of Jews were killed and indubitably these onslaughts were deliberate government policy. Since then the Jews have diffused and dispersed. *Today, those that emigrated from Eastern Europe enjoy residence in every state of the Union, with millions living in New York and the least in Idaho, with maybe one or two!*

The train conductor saw Harry Gold hiding between the seats in a Pullman car. "Let me see your ticket, sir," he requested. "I don't have a ticket, Mr. Conductor," was the response, " I can't afford one, 'cause I'm very poor."

"Everyone has to have a ticket, sir," Gold was told. "I'll

have to put you off at the next station."

"Please don't do that; my daughter is getting married in Chicago tomorrow and I must get to the wedding." Feeling sympathetic towards Gold, the conductor approved free passage this one time and wished the bridal couple good luck. He then moved on.

He challenged another man he found hiding in the dining car for a ticket. "I can't afford a ticket," the conductor was told. " The only reason I'm on this train is because Harry Gold invited me to his daughter's wedding."

If a Jew likes something, he can't wait to relate his pleasure to another Jew. Invite one Jew to a new restaurant; have him enjoy the food and ambience and then watch new crowds appear and noshes disappear. The Greenhorns' taste of freedom opened the floodgates of immigration when favorable comments were disseminated to relatives still in the old countries.

It is important to distinguish between the branches or denominations of the Jewish people. The Jews that settled into Germany, Austria, and Bavaria are referred to as German Jews as well as Ashkenazim together with the other European Jews, not including Spain, Portugal or Italy. This includes Latvia, Lithuania, Poland, Rumania and Russia. The term is derived from the word, "Ashkenaz" a country adjoining Armenia and Euphrates. In can be found as an ancient kingdom in the Bible, Genesis 10.3. It is the oldest Hebrew word used to designate Germany or central Europe Those from Spain, Portugal and Italy are Sephardim. The word Sephardim probably is derived from Hispania, Latin for Spain.

There are a few Oriental Jews that came from Africa, Syria, and Palestine. While 85 per cent of all Jews living today are Ashkenazim, Sephardic dialect is the most common in Israel.

Germans, Austrians and Bohemians comprised the majority of Jewry in America until the mass immigration occurred. They resented the onslaught of the Russians and Polish that came by the thousands to escape government-sanctioned attacks. It is estimated that two-thirds of New York Jews in 1879 were German. These German Jews had integrated themselves economically by becoming doctors, bankers, department store merchants and industrialists. They had spent their time and energy anxious to be absorbed into the American culture only to be unbalanced by their Russian brethren, who were made up of orthodoxy and ultra orthodoxy.

"Where words fail, music speaks." - Hans Christian Andersen

The German Jews were not alone in cultural and the arts. Jascha Heifetz, Lithuanian born immigrant, became a United States citizen in 1925. Awarded a myriad number of musical awards, he became a world-renowned violinist who received a Grammy Lifetime Achievement Award.

Isaac Stern was another brilliant violinist who was born abroad. He gave concerts throughout the world and was acclaimed in Russia for his musical achievements.

The third member of an illustrious musical group was Vladimir Horowitz, an immigrant from the Ukraine. He rendered a limited number of piano concerts but was acclaimed by some as the greatest pianist ever to have played the keyed instrument. Not only did he perform brilliantly but he composed music as well.

The three musicians brought considerable pride to their immigrant brethren. Their artistic contributions in music gendered pride in immigrant Jews and encouraged them to sharpen their natural talents.

Proud of their own achievements and history in America, the German Jews teased the new arrivals on many occasions. "My ancestry goes back to Saxon Kings," Fritz bragged to Chaim. "How far back does your ancestry go?" "I don't know," bantered Chaim, "Our family biographical records were lost in the big flood."

The Germans felt embarrassed by the outdated, old-fashioned clothing and the slovenly baggage of the newcomers. But despite the disdain of kinship displayed by the German Jews, the Greenhorns passed scrutiny and melted right into Americana. They had considerable self-respect , endurance and the desire to be accepted.

The grammar schools of the Jewish quarter are overcrowded with children of immigrants. The poor laborer will pinch himself to keep his child at college, rather than send him to a factory to contribute to the family's income. - Abraham Cahan, Atlantic Monthly, July, 1898

The majority of immigrants started with nothing and had most of nothing when they came here!

The Greenhorns' contributions and those of their descendants to medicine, science, entertainment and law are indelibly impressed in history. They survived tyranny and torture and earned their right to learn and contribute to their new society. They attended classes and enrolled their offspring in Universities. Yeshiva College was founded in 1920 and subsequently became a University including graduate and medical schools. The New York Public Library installed a Jewish Division.

Little Sammy Schwartz, the Greenhorn, entered into the library and asked the librarian for a hamburger, French fries and and a bottle of Coke. "Sir," she told him, "this is a library." "I'm sorry," little Sammy responded and added in a whisper, "sh, I'll have a hamburger, French fries and a bottle of Coke."

Jacob Schwartz walked into the personnel office of a large company with newspaper ad in hand.

"I vant to talk about dis ad," he tells the interviewer.

"Are you under 40 years of age?" he is asked.

"No, I'm 56."

"Are you over six tall as specified in the ad?"

"Me? I'm about five and one-half feet."

"Can you operate difficult office equipment?"

"Not me."

"Sir, why are you here? You don't fit any of the specifics in the ad," he was asked by the interviewer.

"I only came to tell you 'on me you shouldn't count!'"

It would be remiss to omit the name of Henrietta Szold (1860-1945) in an essay covering Russian Jews. She was born to Hungarian immigrants and taught Russian immigrants Torah and Talmud as well as English. She founded the Isaac Baer Levinshon Literary Society from which the first night school for immigrants was inaugurated.

In 1899, she produced the first "American Jewish Year Book." She is also credited for having founded Hadassah Women's Organization.

Sammy Michaelson was a born loser. He never did anything right. Girls ignored him. He went to the library and took out a book with the title "How to Hug." He discovered later that it was the fifth volume of the Encyclopedia.

Because Jews do not have a central authority for their members, the immigrants branched out to all the forms of Judaism in America: Reform, Conservative, Orthodox, Ultra Orthodox and Reconstructionism. Most temple congregations operate autonomously with their rabbi being the total religious authority.

Reform Judaism

The Reform Movement originated in Germany and influenced the German Jews in the United States as early as 1840, with the building of the Emanuel Temple in New York City. In time, they modernized the liturgy, eliminated the second day of festivals and the wearing of skullcaps. The Orthodox had been vociferous in claiming that the abandonment of orthodoxy would cause loss of Jewish identity.

A fraternal feeling existed between the observant greenhorns and the reform despite caustic exchanges between the two groups. Reform Judaism was considered "a religion of convenience" by the immigrants while reform Jews looked at orthodoxy as an obstruction to American acceptance.

Reform Judaism's formal indoctrination shifted to the United States in the middle 1800s, with a modification of Orthodoxy. They introduced organ accompaniment, and offered prayers in English that the Orthodox condemned as theatrics. The Reform favored culture rather than ritual and subscribed to "The Israelite," edited by Rabbi Isaac Mayer Wise in Cincinnati, to keep abreast of the Reform flow. It is important to mention the Columbus Platform that was a statement of principles obligating Reform Jews to aid in Israel's preservation as well as observance of the Sabbath, festivals, customs, symbols and the use of Hebrew.

It has been said of the Reform service that "if you attend before it's over, you're on time."

For the purposes of this light treatise, Reform Judaism as we know it began with the Pittsburgh Platform in 1885, where fifteen rabbis established guidelines for the next fifty years. It is recognized that the genesis of Reform began previously in Germany, but the Pittsburgh platform gave it understandable substance and definition. There was a reform Rabbinical Conference in Philadelphia, five years after the Civil War, that was led by David Einhorn, a Greenhorn rabbi originally from Hungary. He authored a prayer book that eventually found its way as the popular

Union Prayer Book. However, the Conference produced little in the way of Reform ideological academics.

On the high holy days of Judaism, the temples are generally over crowded, necessitating the sale of seats to congregational members and to assist the temple treasury. It has been suggested that the Ortho-dox award the expensive tickets for seats near the ark while the reform charge more for those near the exits.

Rabbi Bernard L. Levinthal, spiritual leader of the Ortho-dox, and Rabbi Joseph Krausekopf kept a distance from each other in Philadelphia but did unite to promote war bonds. Philadelphia maintained social barriers to exclude Jews. The German Jews heeded these barriers as well. Their attitude led to the anti-Zionist American Council for Judaism.

Rabbi Jacob Voorsanger, head of the largest Temple in the West, Emanu-El of San Francisco, felt that Yiddish as a literary tongue was a drawback to the progress of the Jew in both Eng-land and America and should be abandoned.

To the Jews at the time, Philadelphia was the City of Brotherly Love - Cain and Abel.

The Pittsburgh Conference, not to be confused with the Philadelphia Platform, referred to Judaism as a religion and not a race or nation. It emphasized ethical culture but rejected ritual and devine revelation.

As the Reform platform took place in Pittsburgh, the Orthodox felt

*it was a strategic city with which to drown the Reform concept. Pitts-
burgh straddles the Monongahela and Allegheny Rivers that in turn
form the Ohio River.*

Another esteemed Reform movement leader was
Stephen Samuel Wise, who was extremely active in political as well as Zionist causes. He was one of the founders
of the American Jewish Congress in 1914, and what is now
known as the Hebrew Union College. He immigrated as
an infant from Hungary.

*When a Reform Jew was asked if he attended temple services regu-
larly, he replied, "Of course, I never miss a Yom Kippur!"*

At the time of the mass immigrant invasion, the German
Jews felt cultural retrogression and personal resentment
that reigned initially and then subsided when they realized
that they would have to intermingle and serve the Greenhorns as doctors, lawyers and retailers.

Ironically, it is to the credit of the German Jews that pre-
ceded the mass immigration that the newcomers blended
into Americana so easily. They established institutions to
assist them in obtaining employment, living quarters,
recreation and even burial grounds without aid from the
government.

A German financier, Baron de Maurice Hirsch, contributed
millions to assist the Russian Jews coming to America. He
stressed educating the immigrants in agriculture and handi-
crafts. In 1891, he founded the Jewish Colonization Association
to assist in resettling the immigrants.

In 1936, the World Jewish Congress was established, committed to the principal that all Jews are responsible for each other. Unlike today, there were no government entitlements and assistance programs to assist in their preservation.

Most of these arrivals went into the trades, sweatshops, factories and small stores. Compared to their original countries, America was the land of opportunity, and they availed themselves of it on their own.

America is the land of opportunity if you're a businessman in Japan. - Lawrence J. Peter

Conservative Judaism

A large number of immigrants were attracted to Conservative Judaism with the establishment of the Jewish Theological Seminary in New York City. Its founder was Sabato Morais, an Italian immigrant. He originally had been a member of the Reform Movement but his conscience was disturbed by their total disregard of kashruth and other traditional ways of the fathers. Following his demise, Cyrus Adler, an American born Jew, rekindled the interest in Conservatism. He felt that the Russian Jews were detrimental to acceptance of Greenhorns by Americans, and he created a plan to Americanize them through the Conservative movement. He was determined to find a leader with whom to accomplish the concept.

His group selected a Rumanian immigrant, Shneur Zalman, as head of the Conservative Jewish Theological Seminary. Zalman later changed his name to Solomon

Schechter. He was a lecturer in Talmudics at the University of Cambridge, England achieving fame for his identification of early manuscripts of Ecclesiastes, found in Egypt.

Definition of a Conservative Jew–An Orthodox lite

Jewish Socialists helped the immigrants out of the sweatshops through their Union efforts. These socialists were for the most part anti-Yiddishkeit and attempted to disassociate their members from ritualistic Judaism. Paradoxically, they not only encouraged the Yiddish language but conducted classes for its use. While the immigrants did join the Unions, they refused to surrender their credos and traditions. Their reluctance led to the eventual demise of the Jewish Socialistic movement. Oddly, the Workman's Circle (Arbeiter Ring) structured by the socialists boasted more members than the Zionists. It encouraged membership by its support of cultural activities and Yiddish speaking schools.

The Workman's Circle was charted in 1900 to promote Jewish culture and what they termed "Social Justice." Most of their original membership were American workers wilting in sweatshops, causing the group to gather support from an alliance with the American Labor Movement.

We've been creeping closer to socialism, a system that someone once said works only in heaven, where it isn't needed, and in hell, where they've already got it. - Ronald Reagan

The immigrants insisted their offspring retain and rely

heavily on Scriptures, the Talmud and other religious literature in addition to public education that sustained them during their previously threatened existence. This was out of loyalty and tradition to their heritage and a reserve against rejection. Indubitably, the Torah and Talmud together with religious commentaries and constant learning kept their minds sharp throughout the ages. Denied advanced education in Eastern Europe, they made certain their children went to medical, dental and law schools in America. Many private colleges and universities established quotas to limit the number of Jewish students; so the Jews created community organizations, clubs and associations for self-help and mutual benefit. Crime and delinquency were rare.

It has been estimated that Jewish students comprised almost ten percent of the college enrollment in the early 1900s, although they were only two percent of the population. The Jews attended public colleges and universities as the private ones established quotas to limit Jews. Most hospitals did not admit them to internship, forcing the Jewish population to erect hospitals for the expressed purpose of providing internships for Jews. Gentiles were given equal opportunity.

A Jewish Hospital, Beth Israel, was founded in 1890, in New York City and another in Atlanta, Georgia, in 1901, to accommodate Jewish interns and to provide food acceptable under Jewish dietary discipline. This was about the same time that the Hebrew Free Loan Society made its debut to aid those in need.

The Dean of Men addressed the fraternal freshmen at the Univer-

sity during the orientation seminar.

"Men, you are hereby admonished not to enter the coeds' dorms without specific housemother's permission. Any of you caught inside will be fined $50.00 for the first offense and $100.00 for the second. Any questions?"

Whereupon, Sammie raised his hand. "Sir," he asked, "how much for a season's pass?"

In his essay "The Immortal Jews," Mark Twain wrote the following.

"He is as prominent on the planet as any other people, and his commercial importance is extravagantly out of proportion to the smallness of his bulk. His contributions to the world's list of great names in literature, science, art, music, finance, medicine, and abstruse learning are also away out of proportion to the weakness of his numbers. He has made a marvelous fight in this world, in all the ages; and has done it with his hands tied behind him."

The Orthodox

A priest was bemoaning a very sore tooth when he spotted a sign for Dr. John Lawrence, DDS. "Thank the good Lord," he thought to himself as he walked in for dental care.

"Father," said Dr. Lawrence, " you have an infected tooth which I can fix to alleviate the pain." Following the procedure, the priest thanked the dentist and asked, "How much do I owe you?" "Nothing," replied Dr. Lawrence, "I don't charge the clergy."

"Thank you, you're very generous," said the priest. The next day he returned with a rosary as a gift for the dentist.

As luck would have it, a Presbyterian minister walked down the same street concerned about a toothache, when he spotted the sign of Dr. Lawrence.

"Thank the good Lord," he thought as he presented himself to the dentist. He was told that his dental problem was not severe and a simple extraction would eliminate his discomfort.

Following the procedure, he inquired as to the cost of the extraction, whereupon he was told, "I don't charge the clergy."

In appreciation, he returned the next day with a bound New Testament that he presented in appreciation of the dentist's generosity.

A week or so later, a rabbi was walking down the same street, when he, too, felt ache in his mouth. Going in to see Dr. Lawrence, he was told that he had a filling missing and a simple procedure would remedy the ache. Following the removal of the pain, he inquired as to the cost. "Nothing," stated the dentist, "I never charge the clergy." "Thank you for your courtesy he told the dentist." The next day he returned with another rabbi!

It is extremely difficult to define Jewish Orthodoxy as there is disagreement over how precisely the Torah reveals the presence of G-d. How inclusive is the Talmud? How literal can one be in interpreting the Oral Law? All of Orthodoxy believe in the Revelation but interpretation varies within the Orthodoxy as there is no central authority to interpret for all.

Each synagogue ruling body was and continues to be sovereign unto itself. For the purposes of this treatise, Ortho-doxy is a term of traditional Judaism. This would include any Jew who obeys Torah, Talmud and the Shulchan Arukh as interpreted by his own rabbi. Some approve modern dress; others do not.

The Orthodox abstain from eating on Yom Kippur, Tisha Bav, Purim Esther and Tammuz 17th. However, it would be totally incorrect to say they live in the *fast lane!*

There were some common organizations to which these synagogues belonged but they were not bound by outside affiliations. Traditions and practices varied with modifica-tion by the immigrants. The small Rabbinical Assemblies used different prayer books contingent upon the respec-tive rabbi's selection.

Most immigrants came as observant Jews having been raised in close ghettoized areas where they were embar-rassed to wander from Jewish disciplines and ethnic iden-tity. As they accustomed themselves to the American way of life, they varied in their observances. This was particu-larly true of Kasruth (dietary laws). Freed of ghettoized ex-istence and anxious to be accepted into Americana, many of the Greenhorns abandoned the dietary laws. A goodly percentage maintained kosher homes but ate in non-ko-sher restaurants.

One of these immigrants asked the rabbi if keeping ko-sher at home but eating out occasionally at non-kosher restaurants would jeopardize his eternal life. "I don't know about you but at least your dishes will wind up in heaven," the rabbi replied.

PART FOUR

One of the surgical interns said he would never operate unless he really needed the money

A student nurse asked her instructor how to wash the genitals.
"Same as the Jews," came the response.

A Jewish physician, Abraham Jacobi (1830-1919), fondly called "the father of American pediatrics," served as president of the American Medical Association. This was about the time that a superb reputation of Jewish doctors emerged in America. Jewish physicians ironically were excluded from social organizations but their offices were filled with gentile patients.

Albert Bruce Sabin (1906-1993), virologist, immigrated to the United States in 1921 from Bialystok, Poland, and achieved a medical degree from New York University ten years later. He along with Jonas Edward Salk (1914-1995), physician and epidemiologist, are credited with substantially eradicating poliomyelitis. Salk contributed an inactivated vaccine against polio while Sabin developed an oral attenuated vaccine.

Vaccination by needles must be fine. I never saw a sick porcupine!

Dr. Salk was awarded a citation from President Dwight D. Eisenhower and a congressional gold medal for "great achievment in the field of medicine." It is a known fact that he refused all cash awards for his vaccine effort. He has been quoted as saying, "The reward for work well done is the opportunity to do more."

Jerry Krank called his doctor for an appointment and told the receptionist that he felt quite ill. "I can give you an appointment three weeks from today," she responded after checking the schedule.

"But I feel awful," pleaded Jerry. "Can't you do any better?" "No, she replied, "The doctor is a very busy man."

He tried to persuade her by describing his serious symptoms but to no avail. She would not provide an earlier appointment.

Accepting the date and time she scheduled, Krank appeared three weeks later, only to be severely admonished by the doctor that the symptoms were critical and he should have come in sooner.

Karl Landsteiner, (1868-1943) an immigrant from Hungary, won the 1930 Nobel Prize in physiology for discovering main types of human blood. His process allowed for safe transfusions. Dr. Landsteiner also is credited with discovering the Rh blood factor, along with colleagues Philip Levine and Alexander Wiener.

Leo Sternbach is a chemist who emigrated from Poland when he fled the Nazis in 1941. He achieved fame in the 1960s by developing the anti-anxiety pill, Valium. It is claimed that billions of these pills labeled "the most prescribed drug" have been sold.

A woman confused her Valium pills with her birth control pills. As a result, she had ten children but she didn't care.

Jewish American Nobel Prize winners also include Jerome Friedman, Leon Lederman, Melvin Schwartz, Jack

Steinberger, Steven Weinberg and Richard Feynman, in physics: Stanley Cohen Joseph Goldstein, Baruch Blumberg, and Selman Waksman in medicine. Milton Friedman and Harry Markowitz won the award for economics.

Jews have contributed substantially to science and the arts. Although Jews make up less than one percent of the world population, they have been awarded twenty-six percent of the Nobel prizes for scientific research.

The study of economics will not keep one out of the bread line but at least, he'll know why he's standing there. - Author Unknown

Considered the most eminent scientist ever, Albert Einstein was best known for his theory of relativity, which introduced scientific innovations into research of space, motion, time and gravitation. He is credited with introducing the nuclear age.

In 1933, the Nazi government of Germany deprived him of his citizenship while he was on the staff of the Institute for Advanced Study in Princeton, New Jersey. He became an American citizen in 1940, and resided there until his death in 1955.

He was a Zionist and was considered, though he declined, for the presidency of Israel for which he claimed personal incompetence for the position.

A biography indicates that Einstein did not start talking until he was five years old. When the scientist was queried about the oddity, he responded with," I had nothing important to say!"

Isidor I. Rabi is an immigrant scientist known for his development of the magnetic resonance method used to study the structure of atomic spectra. It can also be assumed that he is equally famous for his name appearing myriad times in crossword puzzles. Rabi was awarded the 1944 Nobel Prize in physics and was one of the scientists on the atomic bomb project.

Heaven forbid indiscriminate use of nuclear weapons. It will prove that all men are cremated equal.

There have been many notable names in law as well as physics and medicine.

It is interesting to note that while more than half of the practicing lawyers in New York City were Jewish in the early 1900s, few were in law firms.

A law firm was founded in New York City that provided a battle of wits: Horowitz, Lefkowitz, Rabinowitz and Abramowitz.

There have been several esteemed Jewish judges on the Supreme Court, including Louis Brandeis, Benjamin Cardozo, Felix Frankfurter, Arthur Goldberg and Abe Fortas. Today, there are two, Stephen Breyer and Ruth Bader Ginsburg.

One who belongs to the most vilified and persecuted minority in history is not likely to be insensible to the freedoms guaranteed by our Constitution, but as judges we are neither Jew nor Gentile, neither Catholic nor agnostic. - Felix Frankfurter

Frankfurter was an immigrant arriving in 1894, from Austria. He became a citizen and graduated from Harvard Law School where he served as associate justice for almost 25 years. He also taught law at Harvard University. President Franklin D. Roosevelt appointed him to the the Supreme Court of the United States in 1939.

Louis Brandeis served as an associate justice of the Supreme Court of the United States from 1916 to 1939. He was the first Jew to attain this high office. He was a strong advocate for a concept granting the sole right to Congress for resolving federal legal issues, not the Supreme Court. He deserves credit for initiating minimum wages for working women and supporting child labor laws. It's interesting to note he is better known for his court dissents than agreements.

Arthur Joseph Goldberg, born in 1908, was appointed to the high court by President John F. Kennedy in 1962. He later served as an ambassador to the United Nations. His real fame was as general counsel of the Congress of Industrial Organizations (CIO) and of the United Steelworkers of America in 1948.

The word "judge" reminds me. Never judge a man by his clothes. Judge him by his wife's clothes.

One of the most esteemed artists and painters was Marc Chagall (1887-1985). He was born in Russia, of Orthodox parents, moved to France in 1910, and later came to the United States for a short time. He was known for his surrealistic art, expressionism and cubism. He painted many works of Jewish persons and scenes and folklore; the most famous arguably is The Praying Jew that hangs at the Art Institute of Chicago. He also did a ceiling painting for the Paris Opera and murals for the Metropolitan Opera. Many of his lithographs are sold through Jewish Community Centers and temple gift shops.

As he was born an Orthodox Jew, I wonder if he painted from right to left.

The financially desperate times of the early 1900s are remembered and duly recorded. Many Jews settled immediately in New York and Pennsylvania. Thousands of Jewish settlers became traveling peddlers and ventured into areas across the United States. The new arrivals dispersed into small business ventures in a big way. From there, it was a natural advancement in status to own stores.

Proprietorships had been denied in the old country and venturing into retail selling didn't require formal education. Start-up capital was negligible. The immigrants became entrepreneurs almost immediately upon arrival in America having been forbidden proprietorships in their native lands. Psychologists refer to this as the "Forbidden Fruit " theory, where the forbidden becomes an allurement.

Jews expanded into every facet of their new country and became leaders and principals.

Samuel Gompers, a Jewish emigrant from London, England, became founder and president of the International Ladies Garments Workers' Union. It was the first real effort to eradicate "sweat shops." *The Union acronym, ILGWU does not mean "I Love Girls With Umph!*

Gompers later became president of the powerful AFL.

Many Greenhorns rented horses and wagons to peddle their wares, everything from fruit to rags they called, "Schmatas." (Another definition for schmatas -"dresses your husband's ex wears.") They were referred to as hawkers, hucksters, peddlers and junk sellers.

Dear G-d. I know that under Your master plan, You will provide; but why can't You provide until You provide? - Anon

Most contemporary American Jews are not familiar with the Pale of Settlement, an enclosed district that consisted of approximately one million miles occupied by mostly Jews. It was territory annexed from Turkey in the late 1700s, with perimeters established by the Russians to allow Jews residency and colonization away from the Russian inhabitants. The original Pale of Settlement was a result of a Catherine II Imperial edict some 68 years earlier. It is estimated that it contained approximately four million Jews by 1855. The Pale was abolished after the Czarist regime in 1917. The myriad number of pograms motivated and expedited the Russian Jews' emigration to the United States between 1881 and 1914. It may well have been the single reason for the mass movement. Jews were restricted in several areas that included occupations, agriculture and residence. They were denied the ability to travel outside the Pale or to attend universities. They were leaseholders of the land they lived on but not owners. It was at best an expansive ghetto.

Because of Papal decrees restricting Jews to trade in used goods, Jews became peddlers in old clothes, tobacco, utensils and rags, occupations they brought with them to the United States. The Yiddish word "schmatas" became part of the American colloquialism. Their empirical background in peddling enabled the immigrants to subsist and survive in America.

"Paula, I want you should know I have a date with Yankel Kline tomorrow," Bessie told her.

"I know Yankel, I went out with him Saturday night," replied Paula. "He took me for a dinner and a show and then he took me home. When I opened the door, he threw me inside, tore at my clothes and wrestled me to the floor."

"That's awful," said Bessie. " Paula, my date is tomorrow, what should I do?"

"Wear schmatas!"

The Pale was extended to permit peddlers and other merchants to pay a fee so they could vend their wares. As a result, peddling became the sole source of income for many Jews. It may have been the most chosen occupation engaged in by immigrant Jews in the first five years in their new country.

Immigrant Jews, and or/their progeny, with the most modest means, inaugurated retail outlets that prospered and are respected in the retail business to this day. Included are Lazarus, Gimbel's, Bloomingdale's, Lauren, Lehman Sachs, Goldwater, Stern's and many others. Zahre's was originally titled Zaher Bilig (Yiddish term for very cheap).

The name was subsequently reduced to just "Zayre's," making it easier to remember. It should be noted that Macy's was founded by gentiles and subsequently purchased and expanded by Isadore and Nathan Strauss in 1887. Benjamin Bloomington was an immigrant who came from Bavaria and succeeded in hiring over 1000 employees in just 15 years.

Here is a gentile joke. James Page walks into the men's shop at Bloomingdales and says, " This is a great jacket. How much is it?" The salesman responds, "$750.00." Page says, "Ok, I'll take it."(No negotiating).

The Home for the Jewish Aged (1899) had Jacob Gimbel as its first president. He and other Jewish retail icons were extremely active in Jewish events and institutions.

Jewish merchants were furious in their endeavors to sell. They didn't recognize the accepted seasons: fall, winter, spring and summer. Their format was simple: buy wholesale and sell retail but call retail wholesale. They knew of only two seasons, busy and slack!

Because sales were voluminous during the Christmas season, I'm surprised none of the successful Jewish retailers didn't think of having an express line for Jewish customers.

Sidney Glass went to work for a window shade company at entry level. He worked diligently and contributed many profit-making ideas to the suggestion box.

After one month, the president of the company called him into his executive office. "Sid, I vant you should know that I have noticed your hard work. You come early and leave late every day. Your ideas are have brought in gelt. You show interest in the business. So you'll be happy to know I have decided to make you a vice president after only one month. You're being made a boss before a lot of other workers. Understand that this is highly unusual. Normally, it takes years" "Thanks, Dad," responded Sid.

A Greenhorn lady in a department store asked for directions to the department displaying baby powder.

A clerk who was obviously bow-legged obliged the request by telling her, "Walk this way and I'll take you right to it." "If I could walk this way, dolling, I wouldn't need the baby powder," came the response.

Mama - Papa kosher bakeries, fish stores, butcher shops, delicatessens and grocery stores appeared in abundance almost immediately following the vast immigration. These were specialty shops created to provide the many new-comers who maintained orthodox dietary laws with kosher foods, household supplies and other demanded accommodations.

The bakeries would close early on the Sabbath eve with ovens being restarted after the Sabbath in order to have fresh items Sunday morning. Many of the stores would be open from Saturday dusk to midnight to accommodate the ambitious and hungry consumer. The best selling products were braided challah (festival bread), rye bread, pumpernickel, bagels and Kaiser rolls. The origin of bagels is unknown; although it is claimed they have been in existence over five hundred years. There is some written evidence that bagels were originally offered as mourning (shivah) food, the roundness symbolizing the continuation of life and death.

Grocery stores were the forerunners of today's supermarkets. The proprietors catered to individuals by stocking ingredients and provisions with which to make old native land favorites. One could buy anything from a yahrzeit candle (memorial light) to spritz seltzer. They did extend credit. In Deuteronomy XV-8, we are commanded to lend "sufficient for his need in that which he wanteth." Interest was not charged for the time lapse

At the family owned grocery, one could buy ingredients to make anything from *gefilteh miltz* (stuffed spleen), to *kneidlach* (dumplings). Manischewitz and Magan-David* wines became the drinks of choice particularly on Passover when the companies advertised "Kosher for Passover," and applied written certification. To the best of the author's knowledge, no one ever sued Manischewitz or Magan-David for excessive imbibing. McDonald restaurant has been sued for causing its customers to become obese, Wendy's also. Apparently no one is willing to step forward and admit intoxication or added pounds occurred on a Jewish holiday.

Groceries, as an industry in the early 1900s, were suspected of false weighing or as the saying went, "laying a thumb on the scale." Jewish grocers, being admonished in the book of Leviticus (19:35-36), "You shall not falsify measures of length, weight, capacity," were trusted completely. They were also careful to seek a fair profit and to avoid excessively charging their customers.

"Alfie," commended Beckerman the grocer. "You have been buying from me for a long time. Don't you think it's time you should pay me something?"

"Beckerman," answered Alfie, "you know I only make a few dollars a week. So to keep all the people I owe happy, I put their names in my yarmulka. When I get paid, I pull out the names one by one and pay until the few dollars run out. However, I want to tell you that if you keep pestering me, I won't even put your name in the yarmulka."

Men's hat stores were everywhere to accommodate a vogue of the time, not only for hats, but to cater to the Orthodox women who wore (shaytels) wigs for modesty.

One store advertised credit for hair buyers-"12 months toupee." (to pay).

Delis were popular with the immigrants, for they accommodated with tasty tidbits from the old country. The delis offered selections of knishes, gefilte fish, creamed herring, smoked salmon, cream cheese, whitefish, salami together with myriad tantalizing forshpieiz (appetizers). Chopped chicken liver was a Sabbath Eve must. Corned beef, while expensive, was a delicacy the origin of which the Jews shared with the Irish. While still popular, it found its way to the cardiologists' no-no list. For dessert, there was only one favorite, halavah.

At the door entrance of most delis, a huge barrel or cask filled with sour pickles was placed to tempt passer-bys. More often than not, there was a poetic sign tacked on the cask, inviting a prospective customer to put his arm into the brine and grasp the delicacy; "Grab a pickle, a nickel a stickel (piece).

Processed foods such as salami and bologna became overnight staples in Jewish delis.

The cardiologist told Lakie Schwartz that his alimentary habits of eating fatty foods had endangered his system. The veins were completely blocked and it was his sad duty to inform Lakie that he had only six months to live.

"Doctor, that's terrible. What am I going to do? Besides, I have no money to pay you." So the doctor gave him another six months.

Some believe that bananas were introduced into the United States by a West Indies Jew, Solomon J. Marks, in 1909. This fact drives me bananas because bananas were in this country long before that.

Abe Grossman was Chief Executive Officer of a non-profit organization. He didn't intend it to be non-profit; it just turned out that way.

Ice cream was unknown to many immigrants from Eastern Europe Their first taste may well have occured following a tonsillectomy in America. It is a possibility the ice cream industry prospered as a result of the medical profession introducing and prescribing the frozen dessert to soothe the hurt for those undergoing the surgical procedure.

Poultry shops proliferated in every Jewish section. The various fowl (chicken, duck, goose) were displayed live, allowing a prospective customer to feel the bird for schmaltz (fat) content. It was then given over to an in-house schothet (ritual butcher) for slaughter. Behind his back, he was referred to as the *malech hamovas* (angel of death). The bird was then placed on a hook for one to flick (pluck feathers). The proprietor charged ten cents to remove the feathers. These being depression years, most customers did their own flicking thereby saving the ten cents to economize.

The majority believed that chicken soup was a panacea for any and all ailments with miraculous healing power. *However, there is no scientific evidence that each time a Greenhorn became ill, a chicken died!*

The Yiddish words for the various fowl are as follows:
Chicken - hun or hundle
Duck - katchke
Goose - gandz

However, the immigrant housewives quickly transformed the Yiddish for the fowl into terms of miniscule description. The word chicken became "hundela," duck "katchkela" and goose, "gandzela." La is the Yiddish suffix for small. It was the housewife's way of implying to the proprietor that his fowl was small and overpriced regardless of actual size.

As their English was not exact, the Greenhorns were often duped and misled into buying tref (non-kosher) products labeled "kosher style" or using Hebrew words. This, in turn, led to state laws prohibiting the practice.

Religious bookstores opened in every neighborhood. Many became centers of Talmudic discussion, as the proprietor was generally a *Talmud Chochem*, (Talmudic Scholar). One prospective customer went in and asked where the self-help section was; only to be told, "My telling you would defeat the section's purpose."

These bookstores were stocked with religious creative artifacts in addition to their many prayer books. *Talaysim* (prayer shawls), *tephillim* (phylacteries), *menorahs* and *mezuzas* in various shapes, were in ostentatious display both inside and out of the store. These proprietors were the originators of the now popular "sidewalk sales."

When the immigrants began to disperse, the new neighbors arrived with different religions. It left the proprietors of Jewish book and novelty shops desperate to replace the lost business.

Hy and Bennie owned a Jewish artifacts store in New York. As their regular customers moved away following a neighborhood trend, their sales diminished to a worrisome level.

"Hy, we got to bring in some religious gentile stock like rosaries, crucifixes, statues and all that goyishe stuff."

"Give a look the Yellow Pages and call a supplier for quick deliv-

ery," pleaded Bennie, "We need merchandise."

Hy obtained the phone number of a local supplier; placed an order for the Christian articles and requested quick shipment. "I'll do my best," the clerk told him. "Can't ship tomorrow, though; it's Shabbos and we are closed on Shabbos."

A skullcap, *yarmulkeh* (Yiddish), *kippah* (Hebrew) or *Yid lid* (Gentile) was and continues to be constantly worn by all Orthodox and a section of Conservative Jews as it denotes reverence for the Almighty and recognizes His constant presence.

When the Goodman twins went to say a prayer over hand washing, the older one forgot to cover his head. His father asked his brother to rest a hand on his head to cover it. "What am I?" asked the twin. "Am I my brother's kippah?"

Morry Good, owner of a hat manufacturing company, asked his son Leml, why he didn't want to come into the family business. "I have to see the world, papa, it's exciting. The hat business is dull," responded Leml. "I'll tell you what I'll do," pleaded the father. "If you stay, I'll promote you to the head of an entire department. You'll be referred to as Leml, VP in charge of Yarmulkehs!"

An Orthodox synagogue displayed a huge sign on its front exterior wall, "Under the same management for over 5763 years."

Abe Klein, an aged Orthodox Jew, was exiting from the synagogue following morning services when a gust of wind blew his hat off his head and down the street.

A passerby, John O'Neil, noting the old man's dilemma, gave chase, retrieved the hat and handed it to Mr. Klein, who not only thanked him profusely but blessed him as well.

Profoundly moved by the blessing, O'Neil rationalized that he was destined for good fortune and went directly to the race track. He purchased a tout sheet and noted that a horse named "Stetson" was listed in the first race reflecting substantial odds. O'Neill associated the horse's name with the old man's hat and determined this horse was destined to win. He bet on "Stetson" and when the horse came in first, he was certain he was truly blessed and on the way to fortune.

In the second race, he spotted another hat name, "Adam," and eagerly placed his entire winnings on it that doubled when the race was made official.

John related his story to his wife, who asked him what happened in the third race. "Well," he told her, "I couldn't find any horse with a hat name, so I bet on a horse that lost badly. I never would have picked the winning horse anyhow. I think he was a Japanese entry with the name of 'Yarmulkeh.'"

Jewish entrepreneurs extended credit extensively as most family budgets were severely deficient. Documentation of customer indebtedness rarely existed. IOUs were not an integral part of the credit lexicon. A man's word was truly his bond. The milk bottle became a savings bank wherein coins were placed and accumulated to pay the merchant creditor at the end of the month. Immigrants did believe in insurance and debit payments of fifty cents tendered to insurance agents who made house calls once a month to collect the remittances.

Vendors did not seek collection of seriously delinquent accounts through the courts but they could persuade one to pay a bad debt by threatening to inform the neighbors of default. A negative credit profile was total humiliation to a Greenhorn, for it violated his reputation completely. One proprietor called his customer and said, "Ernie, when are you going to pay me? I've been carrying you longer than your mother did. *She only carried you for nine months!*"

When Morry Lichtstein was in a car accident and lying in the street, a paramedic attended to him. "How you doing?" he was asked. "Ok," he replied. " Danks G-d, I make a living!"

Jews considered themselves brilliant entrepreneurs and the following often repeated story exemplifies that pride.

Two beggars, occupying a sidewalk next to each other in Boston, were wearing religious icons. One had a necklace with a cross; the other sported a Star of David.

Many people walking by placed money only in the hat of the beggar wearing the cross. The one with the Mogen Dovid received nothing.

A priest approached the beggar with the star and asked, "Don't you realize that you're in Boston, an Irish Catholic stronghold? These people aren't going to drop money into your hat. As a matter of fact, your competitor with the cross is getting an increased amount of money out of spite to you." The star wearer listened courteously to the priest, turned to the beggar bedecked with a cross and said in Yiddish, "Moishe, look who's trying to teach us marketing!"

The Mogen David was chosen to represent the Zionist movement in 1897. Many believe that it was the actual shape of King David's shield.

A myriad number of immigrants went out west as peddlers, a trade learned empirically, to sell to homesteaders, laborers and farmers. They inventoried household goods, clothing and trinkets enabling their efforts to contribute substantially to the economy. The peddlers received knowledge and instruction of peddling in America from Jews who introduced the vocation in the South following the Civil War and as a result of having lived in the Pale of settlement.

Levi Strauss, an immigrant from Bavaria, introduced overalls to homesteaders and laborers. His original cloth was made of canvas; that was later replaced with a strong cotton material from Nimes, France. While the canvas was durable as advertised, it was totally uncomfortable causing Strauss to search for a more suitable fabric. The term for the fabric came from the first shipment to Strauss. The box was marked "de Nimes," (from France). Shortened to denim, the manufactured product fabric took on the freight bundle's addressor's stamp name. In 1873, Strauss became partners with a tailor, Jacob Davis, who suggested the overalls be affixed with rivets to reinforce the seams. They used blue indigo for all their jeans. Today, it is estimated that Levi Strauss and Company is the largest clothing manufacturer in the world.

In 1873, Mendel Teitelbaum joined a Wagon Train and journeyed west on a prairie schooner to try his luck selling to homesteaders. He communicated with his folks by Pony Express, relating a horrifying experience. His wagon train was beset by a group of marauding Indians who encircled the wagons and massacred everyone but him. He escaped by buying a blanket and some beads!!

President George W. Bush, in proclaiming April 22 through 29, 2001 as Jewish Heritage Week, recognized the Jewish community supported the country by settling new territories and cities during America's westward expansion.

The Cherokee and the Seminole Indians referred to the Jewish peddlers as egg and cheese men. To maintain the dietary kashruth, the peddlers, who were not armed, would fill their ammunition pouches with hard-boiled eggs and hard cheese to sustain them until they could return to their selling base on the weekend for kosher cusine.

PART FIVE

I know of a very needy family, the head of which is me.

--Chas. S. Elinsky

It is true that Jews contribute more to *tzedakah* (charity) per capita than any other group. This may be due to the admonishment to avoid an evil biblical decree by offering prayer, penitence and charity. There are several references in the Torah relative to the giving of charity. In Deuteronomy XV7, it is written, "If there be among you a needy man, one of thy brethren, within any of thy gates, in thy land which the Lord thy G-d has given thee, thou shalt not harden thy heart, nor shut thy hand from thy needy brother."

When it comes to giving, some people stop at nothing.-Anon

For their annual temple drive, Abe Chizek tendered a check for $1,000. The treasurer called Chizek telling him that the check was unsigned.
"I know," Chizek said. "I'm donating anonymously."

According to the Unetaneh Tokef prayer that is recited

on Rosh Hashonah and again on Yom Kippur, our respective destinies for the coming year are predetermined and sealed. Our actions and deeds of the previous year have been noted and recorded and a decree is issued by Providence for our earthly journey through the coming year. It is written that prayer, repentance and charity can remove a severe decree.

Because writing is forbidden on these holidays, it was deemed proper to interrupt the holy service, announce a urgent need for money and request oral pledges from the congregants following the Unitaneh Tokef admonition to be charitable.

A synagogue was burglarized and the thieves managed to escape with several thousand dollars in pledges!

The Jewish Welfare Committee held a meeting to discuss collection of unpaid pledges. The chairman displayed various pledge cards and asked the members on the committee if they recognized the names of prospective donors or lived in their proximities to pursue for collection.

The volunteer collectors eagerly accepted cards with promises made to contact for payment. Only one card remained. It reflected the name of Rudolph McDougal with an address in a distant suburb where Jews were not known to reside. No one offered to take the card until the chairman voiced the amount of pledge as $10,000. "We need that kind of money. I'll take the card," offered Jack Cohen. "I'm on the freeway a lot. I'll make it a point to exit one stop earlier; go McDougal's house and request payment. I don't mind going out of my way for this important cause."

Jack accepted the card and true to his promise traveled to the home of the pledge donor. He introduced himself as a collector for the Jewish Welfare Fund and asked for Rudolph MacDougal. "I'm Rudolph," stated the man at the door, "What can I do for you?"

"I'm here to collect the $10,000 you pledged to the Jewish Welfare Fund," Jack told him presenting the card.

"Are you kidding?" asked MacDougal. That's not my card. I never pledged to Jewish Welfare. I'm not even Jewish, my wife's certainly not Jewish, my father is not Jewish and even my zadie, 'Olev Hasholem,' he wasn't Jewish."

Every day, for a year of so, attorney Gil Fagen, dropped a dollar in the hat of Schlomie the schnorer (beggar) who had taken up apparent residence on the sidewalk. One day, Schlomie remarked to Gil that more should be donated due to inflationary times. "I'm sorry," said Gil, "times are tough." "Too bad," responded the schnorer," But if times are bad for you, why should I suffer?"

Several second generation Jews became famous celebrity bandleaders. During the late 30s and the 40s, Americans enjoyed a dance craze and twirled to the music of Benny Goodman, Blue Baron, Mickey Katz, Manny Landers and several others. Today's Rappers and Rock bands look upon those famous Jewish maestros as old hat and uninteresting. I declare to them, "As gentile bands, yours are not that great. Consider that the most successful non-Jewish band in American history was Jesse James. His band may not have won Emmys but it is listed in most American history books.

Benny Goodman (1909-86) was the originator of swing music and nationally recognized as the"King of Swing." He was also one of the first bandleaders to integrate a musical quartet and sextet, introducing Teddy Wilson, Lionel Hampton and other black American musical icons to the musical world. A movie "The Benny Goodman Story" was made in 1956 based on his autobiography.

An immigrant mother entered a room where she witnessed her daughter, Linda, embracing and clinging to her boyfriend. They were involved in gyrations and swivels prompting the mother to yell out, "Shame on you. You're doing such a thing in my house!"

"Ma," responded Linda, "We're only dancing. We just forgot to put on the Victrola music machine!"

It can be said that the immigrants gave birth to American

entertainment. Many of their offspring became celebrities in stage and theater performances.

Al Jolson starred in the " Jazz Singer," the first talking picture. He played the role of a cantor's son who temporarily turned away from his Jewish heritage to be in show business and date a shiksa (gentile girl).

Along with Jolson, Charlie Chaplain, Danny Kaye, Alan King, Gene Wilder and Woody Allen highlight the famous names in entertainment. Were they religious? Not evident although Woody Allen's famous quote might reflect their combined attitude. When asked if he believed in G-d, Allen responded, "If only G-d would give me some sign, a clear sign like making a large deposit in my name at a Swiss Bank."

Alan King mentioned his Jewish heritage in almost every one of his routines. He played the role of a rabbi in several of his movies including, The Infiltrator, A Love Story and Bye, Bye Braverman. He suffered from extreme arthritis that diminished his ability to play tennis, a sport in which he excelled. King busied himself by inquiring of everyone he met if they suffered from arthritis and if so, the remedies they took.

When he asked George Burns, (Nathan Birnbaum) comedian and storyteller, if he suffered from the joint disease, Burns responded with, "Are you kidding? I was the first!" King used many Yiddish expressions in his routines and is credited with creating a definition for the Yiddish word, "Grizza"(gnawing) as "the last turn of the screw." He published a joke book of Yiddish anecdotes just pior to his death.

It is interesting to note that the World Book Online Reference Center lists six Jews out of seven named that gained fame and success from early Vaudeville: Jack Benny, George Burns, Eddie Cantor, Al Jolson, Ed Wynn and Sophie Tucker.

Max Fleischer, American motion picture producer famous for animation techniques and popular cartoons, was a Greenhorn born in Galicia. His animation studio produced Ko-Ko, the clown; Popeye, Betty Boop and Superman. Joe Schuster and Jerry Siegel, sons of immigrants, created the extremely popular Superman comic strip.

Another influential Jewish cartoonist was Al Capp who was famous for his Li'l Abner comic strip series, started in 1934. It was a huge success for over 40 years.

Jewish immigrants were aware of sports necessity and established programs through the Young Men's Hebrew Association (YMHA) as far back as the mid 1800s. These, along with Jewish Community Centers, were mainly established by German Jews and spread to the big eastern board cities. They provided cultural, educational and social activities as well as recreational ones.

As these agencies proliferated, they offered special programs in the arts, social work and summer camps.

While the Greenhorns were involved in a myriad number of sports, the prevalent ones were basketball and track. *This was to be expected as Jews have been running during their entire existence.*

Because Jews came from ghettos and small towns, sports, especially competitive ones, were unknown to them. Most Jews were Orthodox; forbidden to participate in Friday night or Saturday events.

The second generation did participate in sports and left an indelible mark. In addition to basketball and track they involved themselves primarily in boxing and wrestling. It is conjectured that these sports were acquired as a means of self -defense in neighborhoods that harbored anti-Semitism. Jewish prizefighters date back to the late 1800s. Joe Bernstein was probably the first Jew to fight for a championship title, featherweight. He lost on a knockout but remained an immigrant's pride. He was followed by Louis Wallach, Harry Harris, Benny Leonard, Barney Ross, and Al McCoy (pseudonym for Harry Rudolph.) The 1920 Olympic team had five Jewish fighters.

Max Baer wrested the heavyweight crown from Primo Canera in 1934. He had endeared himself to Jewish fans when he fought and defeated Hitler's favorite, Max Schmeling, a year prior. The fight was stopped by referee Arthur Donovan to save Schmeling from a harmful trouncing. Baer wore a *Mogen Dovid* (Star of David) on his trunks in the fight against Schmeling. He considered himself Jewish although he had only one immigrant grandparent who was Jewish. A theory existed at the time that he claimed to be a total Jew to attract Jewish fans and as a reproach to Hitler. *A rabbi was asked if the Star of David would help Baer in the fight. "Only if he has a solid right hand punch," the rabbi responded.*

Another fighter who wore the Star of David was Barney Ross (Barnet David Rosofsky). He held three boxing titles at one time; i.e. lightweight, junior and welterweight. Oddly, he won the lightweight title from Ray Miller, also a

Jew. Ross' widowed mother, who was Orthodox was vehement in her objections to her son's pugilist endeavors; however he claimed he needed to box to defend himself against street thugs. Ross was also passionate in supporting the oppressed Jewish people under Germany's oppression.

Many second generation Jews distinguished themselves as baseball players. Sandy Koufax was both a Cy Young Memorial Award winner and Hall of fame member. He pitched for the Brooklyn Dodgers (later the Los Angeles Dodgers) and won several most valuable player (MVP) awards.

Hank Greenberg was another baseball superstar. He won two MVP awards and led the Detroit Tigers to two World Series titles.

Two professional football and baseball team owners distinguished themselves by being innovative. Barney Dreyfull, owner of the National League Pittsburgh Pirates, suggested the first World Series and Art Modell encouraged Monday Night Football by using his organization, the Cleveland Browns.

Definition of a football coach: Smart enough to understand the game and dumb enough to think that's all there is in this world.

Mel Gibson's movie "The Passion," released in 2004, was not the first movie to depict the killing of Christ and blaming the Jews. In the early 1900s, there was obvious anti-Semitism in Hollywood. The B'nai B'rith was emphatic in objections to the picture, *Intolerance,* for claiming Jews killed Christ. Anti-Semitism was obvious in many movies until Gentlemen's Agreement in 1947. That picture, more than any other, helped to slow down the bias.

The successful play, "Fiddler on the Roof," was adapted from "Tevya the Dairyman," written by Shalom Aleichem in Yiddish. Isaac Singer .who started out as a reporter for the Jewish Daily forward, authored "Yentl," "The Yeshivah Boy." These three authors are credited for transforming the Yiddish language into literary acceptance.

Singer who emigrated from Poland wrote prolifically about the pogroms in his native country. Paradoxically, in 1978, he was awarded the Nobel Prize in literature in his collected "Stories for Children."

Sholem Asch, also an emigrant from Poland, studied to be a rabbi. All of his important writings have been translated from Hebrew and Yiddish into English. Two of his recognized novels are The Apostle and East River, an important commentary on Jewish life in New York. The popular book, "The Chosen," was written in Yiddish and subsequently made into a movie.

Leon Uris, the son of immigrants, wrote "The Exodus," a book that vividly summarizes the difficulties of Jews in Europe and the founding of the State of Israel. It was an enormous best seller that was subsequently made into a successful movie of the same name starring Paul Newman.

A story is told of a malka (queen) who loved to read books so she could curl up with the pages!

The languages of Yiddish and Hebrew that the immigrants brought with them from Eastern Europe were written and read from right to left. English translations resulted in literary achievement through the writings of these great Jewish authors.

The Jewish Daily Forward, printed in Yiddish, established itself as the immigrants' most popular medium and the butt of a joke. The editor was rushing to publish an issue when suddenly someone yelled out, "There is breaking news coming in. Hold the back page!!!!!!!!!!"

The Forward was edited for almost fifty years by Abraham Cahan. The circulation of this democratic socialistic, labor-minded newspaper reached a circulation of 200,000 in the early 1900s. There were others: Jewish Morning Journal and Der Yidishe Tog that enjoyed a sound readership only to decline after a short time.

Joseph Pulitzer (1847-1911), son of a Jewish father and Catholic mother, was born in Hungary and immigrated to America in 1917. He owned several newspapers including the St. Louis Dispatch, St. Louis Post and The World. His name is esteemed by journalists everywhere as he supported the original Pulitzer prizes for Journalism. He later sold his newspapers to the Scripps-Howard combine.

Jewish newspapers were widely used by kosher fish markets to wrap the merchandise while other newspapers were deemed inappropriate for the purpose. Inexplicably, avoiding other language papers was totally unwarranted.

What do you call a fish with no eye? Fsh.

"Roseala, my dolling," Mike said to his wife, "I'm tired of bickering. Let's go to a nice restaurant; order appetizing meals and make up."

They went to a famous seafood restaurant, The Red Schmaltz Herring, for a conciliatory dinner.

Both ordered the fish special and as Mike was eating, he began to choke on a bone that could not be dislodged. The manager called emergency and a rescue team was immediately dispatched. Unable to remedy the problem, the medics put Mike in a stretcher and proceeded to the ambulance. As they neared the door, one of the technicians tripped, dropping his end of the stretcher. The patient fell to the floor where the impact caused the bone to dislodge. In the excitement, the couple went home without finishing their meals.

The next day, Mike pleaded with Sally, "let's go back to The Red Schmaltz Herring and have the meal we never had a chance to finish. We didn't quarrel, even once."

The two returned to the restaurant and ordered the same meals. As coincidence would have it, Mike began to choke on a bone again. Emergency was called and as Mike was being taken out, Sally cautioned the medics, "Watch out for that step near the door!"

A college student, Phil Fredericks, blind since birth, was invited to a seder given by the family of a Jewish roommate. At the onset of the service, he, along with the others, was given a piece of matzah. Phil ran his fingers over the top attempting to obtain a Braile message. " This must be Hebrew," he thought to himself. "I can't read any of it!"

The immigrants were comfortable speaking Yiddish at home and with friends and neighbors. The language is referred to as mamaloschen,(mother tongue). It is so called because when mama is talking, papa can't butt in!

PART SIX

Philosophy: unintelligible answers to insoluble problems.

--Henry Brooks Adams

The Oakland, California school board, on December 18, 1996, introduced an academic movement to have a language modification for Afro-Americans called Ebonics.

It is not a formal language but similar to the accepted standard with added dialects and colloquialisms.

The purpose of the proposed adaptation was to make it easier for black students to accept English that would include their parents' idioms. Although the movement was subsequently abandoned in California, the concept carried over to Israel where Falashas, members of the Hamitic Tribe of Ethiopia, were welcomed and made citizens. They had been living and practicing the Jewish religion in their old country since antiquity. Some historians have written that the tribe members are descendants of King Solomon's son and the Queen of Sheba. It was extremely difficult for Falashas to adapt and interweave with new customs and language. It remains to be seen if they will want to create a combination language entitled, "Jewbonics."

The Greenhorns had their own expressions. While never titled, their dialect could have been called,"Hebronics." As an example, the English remark made to a son or daughter "It's been a very long time since you called," could have been translated into Hebronics as "You didn't wonder if I'm dead yet?"

Benky Benkowitz called his aunt Sophie on July 21, 1969, the day after astronauts Neil Armstrong and Edwin E. Aldrin Jr. landed on the moon. "Tanta, did you hear about the astronauts?" he asked. "Esther, what's the matter with Esther?" she wanted to know, not able to discern the diction. "Not Esther," he replied, "Astro---Astronaut." "Please, what's the matter with Esther? Is she in the hospital?" "Tanta, please listen," he pleaded, "I said, 'astronaut' not Esther. Two astronauts flew to

the moon yesterday. Isn't that something?" "Nu," she replied, "If you have money, you can travel!"

Good-natured ridicule was thrust at the Jewish immigrants by each other who maintained an accent even after being in the United States for a time.

"Moishe," asked Al, "How was your winter?" "Wonderful," responded Moishe, "I was in Palaam Springs." "Palaam Springs?" repeated Al, "What kind of Ainglish you talk? You've been in this country ten years and you say,'Palaam Springs;' shame on you!" "You're right, Al," responded Moishe, " I meant to say Palaam Desert."

Some immigrants brutalized the English language while others simply disarranged the sentence syntaxes. Myron Cohen exemplified this by telling the story of the customer who complained to the waiter about the fly in his ice cream. The waiter retaliated with, "Can I help it if the fly likes winter sports?" An immigrant attempted to retell the story to a friend that wound up, "Waiter, I got ice cream in my fly!"

Carl Edward Sagan, a first generation astronomer and author, became popular by discussing planets, and astronomy in language easily understood by laymen. His most popular book is the "Dragons of Eden (1977) that deals with the evolution of the human brain. He later taught at Cornell University.

Albert Abraham Michelson (1852-1931) was an immigrant from Poland. He came to America and achieved fame by being the first American citizen to win a Nobel

Prize in physics for optical instrumentation and tandem measurements. He was also a graduate from the U.S. Naval Academy.

In 1802, West Point academy was established. Their first class was fifty per cent Jewish. There were two cadets and one was Jewish!

An esteemed philosopher and psychoanalyst greenhorn was Erich Fromm (1900-1980) from Germany. He was an antagonist of Sigmund Freud's theories, maintaining that instincts determine behavior. He was educated in Germany but came to the United States to lecture and became a citizen in 1940.

Many immigrants retired to Florida. It is said they worked a sufficient length of time to afford Cadillacs, Rolex watches, Gucci dresses and then moved down south where they ate early bird specials to save money. Florida became a refuge for the Jewish wealthy. It permits them to escape from the north during brutal winters and provides an opportunity to flaunt affluence to others left behind. They enjoy phoning those remaining up north to brag about the heat, golf and swimming. The calls always commence with "How's the weather up there?" These calls are only effectuated when national TV reports snow storms in the northern part of the United States. The calls never start with, "How are you feeling?" Northern Jews take revenge by knocking Florida. "Only the aged go there. It is G-d's waiting room. It's nature's oven. A wonderful place to live if you're an orange. Keep the hurricanes."

Floridian temples are usually packed for Friday night services for two reasons. Firstly, the religious service itself and secondly, the social Kiddush immediately following. The Kiddush, that usually provides coffee, tea, punch and assorted cookies, is free and festive.

The service itself is of short duration. Toward the end, the rabbi generally leads a prayer for the seriously ill termed *"Mishaberach,"* in which he names the sick congregants and requests the Almighty's healing. In Florida, the home of myriad senior citizens, the list is exceedingly lengthy. It makes one wonder why the rabbi doesn't read the names of the healthy ones instead. It would consume a lot less time.

Ten men are required for a minyan (religious quorum), but in Miami Beach, only four in Bermuda shorts and white shoes for pinochle.

Jews, as a group, respect all recognized religions. Their arrows of humor are targeted to be funny, not insolent or disrespectful. It is not true that Jews think the sacramental wine served at the Vatican is called, "Popesicola." It is true that the pope should not be labeled as anti-Semitic because Jews are not appointed to the College of Cardinals!

What constitutes Jewish Greenhorn humor or renders it distinguishable from other types? We have expounded on "the masking of pain" as a main ingredient. If that statement were challenged, I would have to admit that there are other sub-stimuli that contribute on a somewhat lesser plane: pride, nostalgia, and sentiment. These require proper mood levels to bring a smile to a Jew's face. There are simple key words that can produce a giggle: halavah, lox, bagels, gefilte fish, blintzes and hot pastrami. In addition, pleasant surprise endings will generate a laugh or two but this is a prosaïc denominator for every ethnic group.

"Nothing great was ever achieved without enthusiasm." - Ralph Waldo Emerson

The immigrants' younger intelligentsia, looking for new trends, involved themselves in professions, industries and the arts previously unexplored by their parents.

Many entered vaudeville as monologists (stand up comedians) and founded the comedy burlesque routines. These included such notable Jewish stars as Joseph Abramovitz (Joey Adams); Benny Kubelsky (Jack Benny); Nathan Birnbaum (George Burns); Melvin Kaminsky (Mel Brooks); Joey Gottlieb (Joey Bishop); Jacob Cohen (Rodney Dangerfield) , Lenny Bruce, Leonard Hacker (Buddy Hackett), Fanny Brice and many, many more. Star performers every one. They made radio increasingly popular with their respective brands of humor. They relied on family relationships and nostalgia as a basis of humor with which to favor audiences.

Ed Wynn (Isaiah Edward Leopold) won the first Emmy Award in 1949 for Best Live TV Show (The Ed Wynn Show). He was one of the first ever to appear in a television broadcast.

Barbra Joan Streisand, noted previously, is a sensational

female singing star, who has brought pride to the entire Jewish community with her many awards including Oscar, Tony, Emmy, Grammy, Golden Globe and others. She wrote, produced and acted in Yentl; (1983), a movie adapted from Isaac Bashevis Singer's story. It concerns a Jewish girl who masquerades as a boy in order to study the Talmud and involves herself in romantic complexities.

Greenhorn Jews found New York City unbearably hot in the summertime. Air conditioning had not been invented as yet. They countered the oppressive heat by establishing small cabinets in the Catskill Mountains where summers are cool.

They rented inexpensive shanties they called *"Kochaleins,"* self-cookers. It was not uncommon for the wife and children to occupy these shanties the entire week with the father appearing on weekends. As affluence developed, Jewish entrepreneurs having prescience built luxurious hotels with incredible accommodations. Jews from all over the United States spent their summer vacations at Catskill Mountain hotels such as Browns, Grossingers, Nevele, and the Concord. These resorts offered everything from extravagant kosher cuisine and hot tubs to nightclub entertainment; all on independent grounds. This beautiful area still invites anyone interested in canoeing, fishing, golfing or skiing.

Most of the hotels kept *Kashruth (kosher)* dietary laws. At one time the Nevele Hotel's chief chef was Chinese. When questioned as to his knowledge of kosher cooking, he replied that he learned it from his *bubbie, aleha hasholem!.*

It is not true that the official language of the Catskills is Yiddish; there's an abundance of Italian also.

Many a Jewish stars obtained basics there. The list includes Jerry Lewis, Myron Cohn, Freddie Roman, Mal Lawrence, Dick Capri, Red Buttons and many more. Its popularity has diminished but the mention of the Catskills immediately tingles nostalgia. Ask anyone who has vacationed at the Catskills and they will invariably talk about the marvelous cuisine, the abundance of desserts and the taste of delicacies. The waiters, who depend on tips from satisfied diners, are known for insisting their guests eat and eat. *There is an often repeated story of the resort guest who was asked how she enjoyed the resort. She commented, "The food was nothing but poison, and such small portions."*

When the resort guests arrived with their baggage together with insatiable appetites, their priority question was "What time is food served?" Inquiries about scenic mountains, night-show entertainment, the golf courses were held in abeyance. It is said that Jews never leave a wedding hungry, a restaurant without "schlep peckels" (doggie bags) or a resort without a prune Danish.

Washington Irving published "Rip Van Winkle," a story of a man who fell asleep in the Catskill Mountains for 20 years. His description of the area helped to make this one of America's classic short stories. Jewish historians thought that Mr. Winkle might possibly have been an Orthodox Jew due to his long beard. However, Irving failed to mention peyes (hair locks) so the research into the protagonist's religion was discontinued.

PART SEVEN

Remember the days when mothers washed the kitchen floor on the Friday before Sabbath, then put down newspapers to prevent walking on the cleaned floor? I would wager that the process was the forerunner of today's wall-to-wall carpeting. There are many Jewish proprietors today, who developed an interest in the wall-to-wall covering business that was born and nurtured in ma's kitchen.

T he ultra Orthodox make every effort to insulate themselves from strange ways. The reason is simple, to avoid assimilation. They assure themselves that their offspring will not be babes in "goyland."

A story is told of a Church group that wished to build next to a Synagogue. The Synagogue trustees granted permission but to insure distinction, they insisted the Church elders erect a sign "Goys R Us."

Theoretically, the network of other religions emanated from Judaism i.e. Catholicism, Muslim, Quakers, etc. Quakers shake or "quake" at the word of their Lord. This well may have originated with Jewish praying that is done with a "shokel." (shaking). It is also interesting to note that

Jews love to *"hondle,"* euphemism for negotiate or bargain. It is done to such a degree that the process is automatically entered when a sale is imminent. In opposition, Quaker merchants claim hondling implies that truth is flexible. Jews claim it is business itself that is flexible. Jews claim failure to negotiate is sinful.

One of the negative aspects of assimilation is losing the ability to buy wholesale instead of retail. When one sees a congregant thumping his chest during Yom Kippur, it may be atonement for having discovered he paid retail on an expensive item.

There is a Hebrew word, "mehirah" (sale) translated as a transfer of existing legal rights from one person to another. It is also used to denote the transfer for a period of time in which was restricted to the Jubilee when it had to be returned to its original owner. The Jubilee was every 50th year. Jewish women use it as an excuse to return Mothers' Day gifts to the department stores within the week following the holiday. To them, any day is Jubilee Day at the local mall!

"Goy" translates as stranger or outsider. Originally came from the Hebrew. As Orthodox Jews are forbidden to light fires on the Sabbath for food or heat, they request a gentile to do it for them. These gentiles became known as Shabbos Goys. The most famous are probably Colin Powell, Secretary of State and Harry Truman, 33rd President of the United States.

A majority of immigrants modified their religion substantially but the rite of circumcision remained immutable and steadfast. The following story illustrates the modification of the process.

A son, their first child, was born to a poor immigrant family living in an inner city tenement. They provided a meager table of cookies for the guests at the bris (Jewish rite of circumcision). When the father asked the mohel, "How much do I owe you?" he was told, "Twenty five dollars."

Finances improved and the family moved to a decent neighborhood where a second son was born. This time, a luncheon was provided for the bris ceremonty. The mohel (one certified to perform a bris.charged $75.00 for his effort.

The family business prospered even more and the family moved to an affluent neighborhood. They were blessed with the birth of a third son. This time they provided a catered dinner prior to the bris ceremony. The father requested the fee of the mohel and was told $200.00., Whereupon the father spoke up,"The first time you charged me $25.00 and I thought that was a little high but I did not complain. The second time you charged $75.00 which I thought was way too high but I didn't object. Now you charge $200.00, why so much?" "I'll tell you," came the response, "In the poor neighborhood, I performed a bris; in the middle class neighborhood, I charged for a circumcision, but in the affluent neighborhood, I performed a schmekelectomy!"

This is a bit of advice. Never take a front row seat at a bris.

Anti-Semitism made Jews very clannish and protective of each other but not quite as exaggerated in the following story. *Rabbi Mendelsohn was driving by St. Stanislaus Church when he gazed at the church's beautiful garden display. His side-glance dissuaded him from looking at the road and his car jolted the rear of Father John's car directly in front of him. Father John sued for damages. The case appeared in front of impartial Judge Aaron Cohen. The judge listened to both clerics and then inquired of Rabbi Mendelsohn, "How fast was Father John going when he backed into your car, Rabbi?"*

Jews do not laugh at excessive slapstick or buffoonery. They prefer wit, cleverness and satire. These together with the Torah are what have nurtured and sustained us these thousands of years. It is as simple as that.

We, as a people, have suffered intolerance since the creation of time; mainly because we are monotheists and therefore different from most other religions. Being diverse engenders fear that, in turn, engenders hate. We believe that we, as a race, were selected to declare the Almighty's dominion, rendering us the " Chosen People." Because of that, Jews have suffered indescribable persecution and attempted annihilation. This has resulted in the tongue-in-cheek prayer, "Dear G-d, I know we are the Chosen People but could you choose someone else for a change."

Being monotheists, we possess minimal knowledge of other religions nor are there many among us who will learn other religions and compare.. We strongly resist conversion. From a religious standpoint, we insulate ourselves and avoid knowledge of other religious factors because of the third commandment "Thou shalt have no other Gods before me." This is borne out in the following story.

Nathan Goldberg received a call from the school princi-

pal. "Mr. Goldberg, I'm sorry to inform you that we have to expel your son, Moishe, due to several reasons. He is disruptive, incorrigible, and academically deficient." "Oy veh!" responded Nathan, "What can I do?"

"Well, if I were you, I would enroll him in a Catholic school where they have good teachers who are strict disciplinarians," suggested the principal. "We're Jewish, wouldn't that make a difference?" asked Goldberg. "No," he was told, "Moishe can drop the religious courses and just study the regular academics.

So Goldberg enrolled his son warning him that these priests are strict.

The first day home, Nate and his son were having dinner when Moishe announced he was going to his room to do homework. The father was amazed; his son hadn't done homework in years. This homework effort was repeated nightly.

At semester's end, Moishe brought his report card home displaying grade marks as all As. "Moishe," asked a gleeful father, "all A's? You never did better than Cplus!" "Dad," responded the son, " just like you told me, these Catholic priests are tough. The first day I'm there I see they have some kid nailed to the wall!"

Here is another example of deficient knowledge of other religions.

Frank Flanagan is discussing his Catholicism with his neighbor, Charlie Levine.

"Charlie, you're a Jew. You don't know anything about us and Catholicism, do you?" he asked. "Yes, I do, answered Charlie, I know all your prayers. Having lived behind your church for 20 years, I hear those prayers over and over again to the point where I know exactly every section and page." "Your full of bull," he is told. Name some!" Charley eagerly shouted back, "B-17, I-3, N-14, G-2, O-5."

Two youngsters were arguing in the school playground. Fritz teased Sammy that Catholicism provided a wonderful hierarchy for their clerics."We have a system of church government in graded ranks," he said. "All the Jewish religion has is one position for a rabbi while we have a lot to reward a priest. He can become a monsignor, bishop, archbishop, cardinal, pope even a saint. Can't go any higher than that!" "Sure can," retorted Sammy, "there's a step above saint and one of our boys made it!"

Three elderly Jews attended a church ceremony where nuns were to marry Jesus for their final acceptance into the convent. The officiating priest, noticing the strangers in the rear pew, asked the altar boy to inquire as to their presence.

Father Dominic welcomes you. Not having seen you in this parish before, he wants to know of your interest in the ceremony." "Tell him," said one of the visitors, "We're relatives of the groom."

The secret of a good sermon is to have a good beginning and a good ending and having the two as close together as possible. - George Burns

When the Jewish immigrants settled down in an area,

they would immediately erect a synagogue as a priority. The intention was to live near each other as commanded by the admonition, "Do not separate yourselves from the community." This was also due to ghettoized existence in the old country. The synagogue was always situated in the center of their populace to insure attainability. Not only did it serve for purposes of worship but as a Hebrew educational institution as well. It provided shared interests and restrained individuals from going in different directions while keeping them focused.

The erection of a synagogue was systematically followed by the construction of a burial plot. As the immigrants dispersed to the south and west, they organized so called "Hebrew Benevolent Societies" to provide financial aid and burial benefits. The first was started in Atlanta, Georgia in 1860. Many of these societies founded in the 1800s flourished and are still in existence today.

"Yossel, do you ever give any thought to what you'd like on your gravestone?" asked Dovid. "Sure," answered Yossel, "I'd like to see somebody else's name."

Automobiles were not common as yet in 1900 as there were less than 7500 automobiles on roads that were terribly rutted. Exodus 20.8-10 commands that the Sabbath be kept holy creating a tradition for the Orthodox not to drive on the day of rest and holidays.

One can always recognize important Jewish holidays. They are the ones on which alternate-side-of-the-street-parking-ban is suspended.

   Credit can be given to Henry Ford, an esteemed pioneer in the automobile industry, for providing mobility to the Jewish community. The automobile enabled them to migrate to the suburbs where they established a myriad number of synagogues. It is paradoxical that Henry Ford, an alleged anti-Semite , unwittingly assisted in substantially increasing the number of synagogues in a thirty -year span. Historians have estimated that there were approximately 2000 synagogues at the turn of the century doubling in thirty years.

   The synagogue was the most influential institution in the immigrants' lives. It was available for prayer, study, food and shelter. The Greenhorns became very attached to their respective temples and when they migrated to the suburbs they obeyed a Talmudic admonition not to sell or demolish a synagogue until another was provided.

   Ford's assembly line produced the automobiles that motivated various manufacturers to mass-produce vehicles. The mobility, thus created, encouraged the Jews and others to abandon their environment that led to suburban migration. In these outskirts, the Americanized immigrants erected modern architectural temples with giant parking lots to accommodate those vehicles that, paradoxically, were not Fords. The industrialist published the Dearborn Independent that angered the Jewish community when he promoted virulent anti-Semitic articles including the Protocols of the Elders of Zion. He did offer an apology subsequently, but the damage had been done. The immigrants withheld patronage from the Ford Company.

Issac was reading the Protocals when his friend, Her-schel, approached him. "Why you reading that anti-Se-mitic trash for, Hersch?" "I'm reading it because it is so op-timistic. It says, 'Jews have all the money; control the banks and the media. It goes further and says Jews produce all the movies.' It sure makes me feel good to read all this won-derful stuff about us."

There is a story circulating about three brothers who of-fered to sell their auto air-conditioning patent to Henry Ford on one condition, i.e. each unit display their common Jewish names. He refused, so the patent was sold to General Motors who stamps each unit with Hi, Norm and Max.

When General Motors, Cadillac Division, announced a recall a 72,000 Cadillacs on Yom Kippur eve, more Jews than ever walked to synagogue the next day.

Most Jews, mindful of disturbing history, generally do not buy Fords, Volkswagens or Mercedes. The sanction also serves as a legitimate excuse for those that cannot af-ford a Mercedes

Some guy hit my fender the other day, and I said unto him, "Be fruitful and multiply." but not in those words. - Woody Allen

The automobile industry urged movement of Jews into suburban areas where they opened retail businesses. New life styles were adapted which in turn led to expansion and modification of Orthodoxy, Reform, Conservative and Reconstructionist Judaism.

Today, one can easily estimate the wealth of a respective Jewish congregation by examining the size of the adjacent parking lot, not by the type of vehicles stored there. If the lot is full of European made vehicles, you can safely bet there is a Bar/Bat Mitzvah, wedding or baby naming rite and gentile guests are attending.

A temple was confronted with a parking lot problem. Baptists attending a church for earlier services in the proximity availed themselves of the temple's parking space. The temple congregants did not want to tow away the Baptists' cars or confront them verbally. They decided to resort to bumper stickers. One Saturday, they stuck a bumper sticker on every car bumper in the lot, "PROUD TO BE JEWISH!" That ended the parking lot problem.

Jews were not welcomed in fashionable suburbia. As they sought advanced education, they were met with strict quota systems. Medical schools in particular established severe restrictions that carried over to hospitals.

If you forget you're a Jew, a gentile will remind you.

Charles E. Coughlin, a Roman Catholic priest, also disseminated "The Protocols of the Elders of Zion" through publication of his magazine "Social Justice" and his weekly radio broadcast that was heard by millions. His effort was supported by the Irish Catholic "Christian Front" that sponsored boycotts of Jewish businesses. The defeat of Nazism, a doctrine of extreme hate, vanquished his efforts and that of other outspoken anti-Semites during World

War 11. America witnessed first hand what malicious hate can create. *His ecclesiastical attire should have had an extended zipper to go up his chest and across his mouth!*

The 1930's depression witnessed the rebirth of the Ku Klux Klan and its uniting with the German-American Bund. *The KKK was not only covered with a sheet; it was full of it.*

There was an interesting story that came over the Internet in May of 2003 stating that New York State Judge Nathan Perlman personally contacted the gangster Meyer Lansky requesting him to disrupt the Bund Rallies but to stop short of any killings. Lansky, according to the item, accepted all of the judge's terms except one: he would take no money. Lansky, stating he was a Jew and feeling sentiment for those suffering in Europe is credited for effectively breaking up one Nazi rally after another. Lansky also took credit for disrupting a Brown Shirt rally in Manhattan. He claimed that fifteen of his men caused the Nazis to panic and run out.

The article also credited Minneapolis gambling czar David Berman for breaking up the virulent anti-semitic William D. Pelley's Silver Shirts by cracking heads and beating Nazi bodies. These gangsters were ruthless in their daily routines but they were ultra sensitive to their racial heritage. It has been reported that Jewish gangster Mickey Cohen agreed to raise money for the American league for a free Palestine. For those interested in learning more of the exploits of these known mobsters, there is a book ironically titled, "But he was good to his mother," by Robert A. Rockaway.

A Jewish gangster was taken to a hospital, having lost a gun battle with his competition. First thing he said after surgery was "I'll kill the guy that put a violin in my violin case!"

Jews abuse themselves because we perceive ourselves as being eternally guilty. As Abraham's descendants, we have continually broken G-d's commandments and a guilt complex has pervaded our lives. We consider the evaluation of life as one of negative thinking about most everything. *Call Rosie Rosenblum; reach her answering device, and you will hear, "I'm Jewish; at the beep, leave the bad news!"*

Mendel Sopich approached his rabbi with a lament. "Rabbi, I painted Joe Goldfarb's house with material that I thinned with water and turpentine. The job will never last. Goldfarb paid me good money and I feel badly. What should I do?" "Well," said the rabbi, "for starters you should repaint and thin (repent and sin) no more!"

You can get used to anything if you have to, even to feeling perpetually guilty. - Golda Meir

Our faith has caused Judaic life to be an on-going contest. We have been forced to feel as if competitors are continuously tormenting us. When agitated, we attempt to get even with the adversary by using wit and mental skills.

Thinking Yiddish (synonymous with being smart) is interwoven throughout our anecdotes. Retaliation through humor can be both challenging and invigorating. It should be pointed out that not everyone is able to emphasize the soul of a joke, yet most people do try.

Israel, an independent democracy since 1948, has been

in constant conflict and struggle with Arabs.They are not the only ones engaged in a struggle. There is fighting going on all over the globe. North Korea versus South Korea; in Ireland the Catholics versus the Protestants; in the Philippines it's the rebels versus the Royalists, the Al Qaeda versus everyone else. *G-d created this crazy world in six days; perhaps he should have taken more time!*

Dovid, sitting on a curb in Israel, kept repeating the number "Eighty- eight." "Eighty-eight, eighty-eight, eighty-eight," when he was confronted by an Arab. "Why are you repeating the number eighty-eight?" he was asked. "Eighty-eight, eighty-eight," the Jew kept on. The Arab became incensed and threatened to harm Dovid unless he revealed his reason for the repetition.

"I'll tell you," said Dovid. " I discovered that when I repeat the magic number 'eighty-eight,' harm won't come to me. I can even cross this major highway, and as long as I say' eighty-eight', I won't have an accident." "Show me," demanded the Arab. Whereupon, Dovid crossed the highway; all the while repeating "eighty-eight, eighty-eight." He then returned safely.

"Will that work for me?" asked the Arab. "Try it," he was told. The Arab attempted to cross the busy highway while muttering the given number. As he approached the midway, an automobile hit and killed him. Dovid then uttered "Eighty-nine, eighty-nine."

An Arab tank and an Israeli tank are going up a sand dune on opposite sides. Neither is aware of the other. They reach the top simultaneously and clash. The Arab jumps out of his tank, arms raised, and yells out, "I surrender, I surrender." The Israeli jumps out of his tank and yells, "Whiplash, whiplash!"

Two Arab women met in the market. "Renya," greeted her friend, Tali, "How are you?" "Wonderful," she responded. "I'm getting married and to a doctor, no less." "That's wonderful," responded her friend, "what's he like." "Well, he's Jewish, an Israeli sabra and orthodox." "Really," gasped Tali, "does his family accept you?" "Of course," answered her friend. "Matter of fact, they're having a big party in our honor. They call it a shiva (mourning period).

In 1967, Israel was involved in what became known as the Six Day War. There was much concern by Jews due to the tremendous number of Arabs versus Jews. One American statesman alleviated their fears by saying, "There are four hundred Arab heads against each Jewish head. Why are you worried? Seems to me, the odds are even."

Israel has been the target of Palestine terrorists since its inauguration as an independent state. Air raid sirens warning the Israeli citizens of pending bombings have been common. Harry Lieberman and his wife Sarah, hearing a siren, ran towards their safe room when she suddenly cried out, "Harry, I forgot my false teeth." "Forget the teeth," yelled Harry, "You think they are going to drop sandwiches?"

In Germany during the horrific reign of terror by Nazis, a Jew was hawking his fish wares in the street. "Herring,

Herring," he shouted, "fat as Goering." Caught by the police, he was hustled off to jail where surprisingly, he was released following a stern warning not to insult the Nazi Field Marshall. He reappeared on the street a few days later where he again advertised his wares. "Herring, herring, same as last week."

This joke was a clever morsel of revenge for all Jews.

We laugh because the Jew had his moment of retribution to hostility.

Jews adopt a protective attitude against the worst by poking fun. There are myriad objections to using the Holocaust as a backdrop for humor. Sensitivity to the genocide is recognized and respected as organized violence by the Nazi Germany resulted in 6 million European Jews being exterminated. However, to totally restrain from humor would violate the maxim that Jews survive by making fun of adversity. Many Holocaust survivors have stated that making jokes kept them alive in the hellish camps.

Ralph Waldo Emerson, in his essay on The Comic, referred to laughter as being provoked by a man in a high wind running after his hat. Apparently RWE wasn't Jewish as his illustration would not provoke laughter to the average Jew. He would rather enjoy the victim's ability to contrive retrieving the hat without exertion. Jewish humor seeks a way around the obvious.

Abe Lefkowitz, unsure of the postage he applied to a package, took it to the post office to be weighed. He was told that the package was too heavy and an additional twenty-cent stamp is required. "That will make it lighter?" asked Abe.

An Israeli soldier, Sgt. Ira Shapiro, on leave, walks in front of Sam's tailor shop displaying a sign in the window, "What do you think; we press clothes for nothing."

Thrilled by the offer, Shapiro enters, announces his need of a pressed uniform and hands his clothes to Sam as he intends to wait for the pressing. After a short time, the tailor hands the uniform back to the sergeant and requests a payment of five sheckles. "Why," the soldier wants to know. "Your sign says, "What do you think, we press clothes for nothing!"

"The sign is not a statement," Sam tells him. "You didn't read it right. It's a two-part question.'What do you think? We press clothes for nothing?'"

"Waiter, I want you should taste the soup," cajoled Levi. "What's the matter with the soup?" questions the waiter. "Taste the soup," Levi told him again. "OK," responded the waiter," but where's the spoon?" "Ah, ha," responded Levi.

Jews do not have manipulative personalities but they enjoy thwarting efforts to convert them, which has been proven difficult over the years. When Bennie Benjamin was approached by a missionary evangelist who stated that Jesus saves, Bennie retorted with, "Big deal; Moses invests."

In Yiddish, there is the expression, "It is difficult to be a Jew." Said because we have so many commandments (613) to fulfill and traditions to adhere. We display reverent behavior for these commandments and traditions, but we enjoy some joshing as well. It has been said that all of the 613 commandments can be found in the first ten.

PART EIGHT

✡ ✡ ✡ ✡ ✡ ✡ ✡ ✡ ✡ ✡ ✡ ✡

Not only does a Orthodox Jew maintain a minimum of three sets of dishes, his house should have two smoke detectors; one in case of a meat fire and one for dairy.

Elinsky

A t the Passover Seder, near the end of the service, it is traditional to open the door slightly for the spirit of Elijah, the prophet, to enter.

The purpose is inherent in the hope that Elijah will make

a memorable announcement: Meshiach (Messiah) is coming. That didn't happen but something memorable did when the Schwartzes opened their door. The cat got out!

Why is this amusing? We have taken a value and reduced it to a subordinate level. Like children, we sense and enjoy independence creating a tendency to be whimsical with a solemn tradition.. We extended some authority to ourselves to loosen from regimentation by phrasing tradition differently and obtained a sense of freedom from religious bindings.

Jews drink sacramental wine following an appropriate blessing. On the holiday of Passover, they may even partake of four or five cups as prescribed in the Haggadah. *Consuming them can lead to problems. "One cup, two cups, three cups, floor!"*

Another tradition is slighted with this jocosity. Saturday, the Bar Mitzvah chanted his Haftorah followed by a speech. In it, he uttered the words, "Today, I am a man." Monday, he returned to the seventh grade.

Jews can poke fun at traditions without really being offensive to those traditions.

What do we do on the following holidays? Here's food for thought! The Internet has displayed it numerous times, in different ways. The following is a consensus.

Rosh Hashanah - We feast. Include apples and honey

Tzom Gedalia - We fast. No apples and honey

Yom Kippur - More fasting

Sukkot - Feast

Hashanah Rabbah - Continue feasting

Simchat Torah - Don't diet; keep feasting

Month of Cheshvan - You must have overdone the feasting. No feasts or fasts for a whole month. Good time to start that diet you promised yourself.

Hanukah - Here we go again. Limit your feasting to potato latkes

Tenth of Tevet - Do not eat potato latkes

Hamisho Osor B'Shevat – Feast on fruit

Fast of Esther - Fast. Not even fruit.

Purim - Feast on pastry that looks like homentashen

Passover - Do not eat anything that even looks like homentashen. Matzoh, moror and knedlach are ok

Shavuot - Dairy feasting-(cheesecake, blintzes, etc.) 17th of Tammuz-Fast. (definitely no cheesecake or blintzes)

Tish B'Av - Very strict diet (don't even think about cheesecake or blintzes)

Month of Elul - End of cycle. Eat or fast.

Jewish immigrant mothers admonished their kids to eat, mindful of meager meals in the old country. It has become a paradigm for these mothers to say, "Eat, eat. In Europe, children are starving." When a hostess asked Pudgie why she wasn't eating, followed by "Didn't your mother ever tell you to eat because children in Europe are starving?" Pudgie replied, "She didn't have to; I always ate everything!"

The following was found in a synagogue newsletter:
Weight watchers will meet at 7p.m. at the J.C.C. Please use the large double doors at the side entrance.

Sophie bought a talking scale. The first time she tested it the scale said, "Will one of you please get off?" I wonder if Sophie removes her earrings prior to weighing herself.

The reform movement was the dominant Jewish influence just prior to the mass immigration phase of the Orthodox and traditionalists. Rabbi Isaac Mayer Wise, an immigrant from Bohemia, founded the Hebrew Union College in 1875. He is also credited with organizing the Union of American Hebrew Congregations in 1873 and the Central Conference of American Rabbis in 1889. He felt strongly that Judaism could not survive in the United States without modification. Under his tutelage, religious services were extremely short and the second day of religious holidays was not celebrated. Reform proponents were often kidded about being open at all on the Sabbath.

Do not confuse Isaac Mayer Wise with Rabbi Stephen Samuel Wise, who was born in Hungary and came to America as an infant. He helped to organize the Jewish Institute of Religion and the American Jewish Congress. He was an ardent Zionist, helping to organize the Zionist Organization of America. He is considered one of the foremost leaders of the Reform movement.

The Reform, under German Rabbi Samuel Holdheim, held that monotheism, ethnicity and morality were to be retained by Judaism with Jewish ceremonies, law and rites being diminished

Reconstructionism is an ideology and philosophical tendency that the Greenhorns didn't commit to. The movement was started by Mordecai Menahem Kaplan, an immigrant from Lithuania, who preached that salvation can be attained in this world; not the next.

He established the synagogue as the central unit for Jews that would include gymnasiums, educational schools, drama, social and fraternal clubs. Kaplan taught that the Jewish religion exists for Jews and that Jews do not exist for the religion. He did not recognize G-d's revelation or Messiah; nor was it necessary for Jews to return to Israel. Kaplan did propose to retain the holidays and rituals. His concept is not easily defined and appealed to several of the cultured but failed to interest the immigrants. However, he was a great Zionist.

I think he would have had more acceptance had he invited the immigrants to the Jewish Center for noshing which could have included blintzes, cholent, gefilte fish, gehakte herring, griebenes and lox.

As Jews were denied store ownership in Europe and Russia, they turned to books and became doctors, lawyers and accountants in limited numbers. The pursuit of these professions can provide sufficient monetary reward. A doctor is what Jewish mothers seek as the ultimate for their daughters as it represents financial security.

The following is an old Jewish favorite. A play on Broadway was interrupted by someone hollering, " Is there a doctor in the house? Is there a doctor in the house?" "Yes, madam," came a response, "I am a doctor." "Oy, doctor, have I got a daughter for you!"

She got her good looks from her father. He was a plastic

surgeon. - Groucho Marx

Goldie Nusbaum prayed to the Almighty and asked for guidance. It appears her daughter, Ida, never called her or sent money. The Master of the world responded by saying, "Look at My empty temples; My children don't visit anymore nor do they contribute generously to charities. I have the same trouble you do!"

The Cantor approached Chaim Klug and greeted him with an enthusiastic, "Shabbat sholem, peaceful sabbath. It's nice to see you. You haven't been present here for some time."

"Cantor," replied Chaim, "How can you say that? I'm an active member in the army of G-d."

"Chaim, don't kid me," chided the Cantor. "You only come to service on the holy days. How can you say you're in the army of G-d?"

"I'm in the secret service," came the reply.

There is a recognized fanaticism by Jewish mothers over the medical profession. To illustrate the obsession, the following story was told.

Hannah meets her friend, Abby, at the market. "Abby, how happy you must be? Your son, Harry, went from Councilman to State Representative to Governor and now is the Democratic candidate for President of the United States. That's incredible. Mazeltov! You must be thrilled." "Not such a big deal," retorts Abby, "my other son, Mendel, is a doctor."

An old Jewish axiom that has been repeated myriad times cautions a person requiring assistance to go the head and not the feet; unless of course, a podiatrist attends to the foot care. Then the axiom does not apply to one's daughter.

On various occasions, the Jewish mother-daughter relationship is questioned and challenged. Becky Gold approached the rabbi and told of her desire to be cremated in the event of her demise. The rabbi explained that cremation is not an acceptable Jewish ritualistic practice and therefore he would not be able to accommodate her wish. "Rabbi," she stated in a firm tone, "I insist on being cremated and my will stipulates that I leave $100,000 to the temple if the wish is fulfilled." "In that case Becky," responded the rabbi, "because we certainly can use the money, let me give the idea some additional thought. I must ask why you wish to be cremated?"

"Well," responded Becky, "I want my ashes to be strewn all over the Famous Shopping Mall making it certain that my daughter will come to visit at least once a week."

The above story also reflects a trend of Jewish stories towards bribing the rabbi. It is unfortunate that assimilation has caused our humor to evolve into a slow but realistic irreverence. Here is one more.

The Ginsburgs approached Rabbi Schlomie with a unique request. "Sir, we are in love with our dog Sam who is going to be 13, and we would like to have him Bar Mitzvahed. We do not have children and therefore it is our one desire."

"Are you meshugah?" questioned the rabbi, "that would be sacrilegious. I won't even consider it." "Sir," said Ruby Goldberg, "We love Sam so much, we would be willing to leave $100,000 to the temple in honor of the rite." "Mr. &

Mrs. Goldberg," responded the rabbi, "Why didn't you tell me the dog was Jewish?"

Our associate rabbi is very young with boyish features. It seems incredulous that he spent years at the Yeshivah. I wasn't shocked when I walked into his office without introduction to find him reading "The Rabbinate for Dummies."

Sabbath morning, Rabbi Engleman called over Eddy Marcus, the head usher. "Eddie, wake up that congregant sitting in the front row." "Why should I?" responded Eddy.

"You put him to sleep Rabbi, you wake him up!"

A Reform congregant approached his rabbi. "Sir, I pray to the Almighty three times a day; and thank Him at every meal. Yet, I barely make a living. My brother who doesn't pray at all, eats trafe (non-kosher) is rich and successful. Why?" The rabbi thought for a moment and then offered the following, "You're a nudge!"

Rabbis do retaliate. A story is told of one receiving a call from the Internal Revenue Service. "Rabbi, did Chaim Goldberg contribute ten thousand dollars to your temple?" asked the agent. "No, but he will," came the reply.

Sabbath morning, Rabbi Berg entered the Temple to find Jack Hinkle at the door passing out sedurim (prayer books) and programs. "Wonderful to see you in Temple, Jack, you haven't been here in quite some time. I'm delighted that you wish to reconnect with the Judaic spirit through meditation and synagogue prayer. I also want to mention how nice of you to volunteer greeting congregants with pass outs." "Rabbi," responded Jack, "I'm here because the judge gave me community service."

PART NINE

Every man gets the wife he deserves

--The Talmud

Indecency and obscenity are rarely interwoven in Jewish anecdotes. Think of it; you don't have to insulate your children from Jewish joke books fearing they might read something too prurient or off color. The Greenhorns brought with them an undeclared sacred pledge not to make fun of sexual relationships. Prurient comedic material was rare and brought responses of disgust. They did, however, affably ridicule marriage as an institution.

Bigamy is having one wife too many. Monogamy is the same thing. - Oscar Wilde

Chaim was on his deathbed and gasping. He said to Becky, his wife, " After I die, I want you to marry Joe."

"Joe," she repeated. "I thought you hated Joe."

"I do," gasped Chaim.

What did Eve do each time Adam returned home? She counted his ribs!

A story is told of Linda Garfinkle who left her husband,

Irv, because of illness. She got sick of him!

In a court proceeding, the Judge granted Rosie Baum a divorce from Jake. She told him that as part of the settlement, she would like to resume her status prior to the marriage. "What was that?" asked the judge. "A widow," she replied.

Herschel Levine, a new Temple Mitzvah congregant calls Rabbi Handlebaum. "Rabbi, I must tell you that my wife, Leah, wants to poison me." "Calm down Herschel, I'm sure you're mistaken," the rabbi tells him. "I'll talk to Leah and advise you afterwards." About three days later, Rabbi Handlebaum called his congregant. "Herschel," he said, "I met with your wife and I have some advice for you. Take the poison."

The most popular labor saving device today is still a husband with money. - Joey Adams

Here is another example. It's an old favorite and worth retelling. Two women are seated together on a flight to New York. The younger of the two asks to obtain a closer look at the huge diamond on the hand of her neighbor. "Madam, that is the largest diamond, I have ever seen." "It reminds me of the Hope diamond or the Diamond of India I saw in the Art Museum. They came with curses."

"This is the Plotnick diamond. It also comes with a curse." "How romantic?" giggles the young gal. "Not so romantic," insists the jewelry owner. "The curse is Mr. Plotnick."

Irving Harris confided to his psychiatrist, Dr. Jeffrey Markewitz, that he wanted to get married but his mother objected to the girls he brought home. It was apparent that she would reject any girl he found attractive. She hated this one and she hated that one. "Well," said the doctor, "try finding a woman that looks like your mom and has her mannerisms. She can't object to one that looks and acts like she does. It would be like hating herself." "Thanks, doc, sure sounds plausible to me," replied Irv.

Taking the doctor's advice, Irv searched everywhere for such a woman. Incredible as it may seem, he finally found one that looked and acted exactly like his mother. He couldn't wait until he introduced the young lady to her for approval. He finally collected sufficient nerve and brought the young lady home only to discover that his father couldn't stand her!

My wife has a slight impediment in her speech-every now and then she stops to breathe. - Jimmy Durante

PART TEN

The bible is also susceptible to chortles. In Genesis XV11-11, Sara gives birth to a son at the age of 95. One wonders if that wasn't past her milk expiration date.

Jews do not make saints of their biblical heroes or engage in idol worship in order to insulate themselves from the third commandment against having false gods. There are quite a few one-liners that will cause a smile or two: Accept the truisms that Adam and Eve raised Cain and that Adam was not Abel. It is also true that Jacob and his son Joseph were dreamers.

G-d spoke to Abraham and instructed him in the rite of circumcision. Abe must have responded, "You want me to do what?"

We do revere and regard Moses with deep respect but like any other human being, he is subject to retrospection. It seems difficult to believe that in the Haggadah, the story of Passover only mentions Moses one time. It refers to G-d and Moses his servant. This is to emphasize that he was only mortal. Consider this. He was a servant of G-d and made mistakes. Had he planned better, he would have led the Israelites to oil instead of desert.

Hebrew schoolteachers, *melamuds,* are exceedingly careful to quote the bible exactly. Unlike the New Testament, which has been rewritten many times, the Old Testament remains unchanged. A teacher of Hebrew Scriptures would never edit or modify the Old Testament. For exam-

ple, can you imagine a rabbi translating *"David slew Goliath" into "the kid kicked the hell out of the big guy?"*

The bible tells us that G-d caused a deep sleep to fall upon Adam, removed a rib and created woman (Genesis 11,21). Adam then said "This is now bone of my bones;

and flesh of my flesh."

The Midrash (explanatory notes and rabbinical commentaries of the scriptures) does not comment on the greeting; but that has to be the least romantic remark since time began. Imagine a man waking up, seeing a woman for the first time since Creation and making that statement! It is not exactly idyllic or impassioned.

Couldn't Adam have thought up a more fanciful statement? It proves that Jewish men, being descended from Adam, as each of us is, certainly are not romantics. Good providers, maybe; romantics, doubtful. What was Eve's response? Zero. The bible does not reflect any reference to her first words. *It does not require any editorial note to state that woman has made up for the obvious silence since then.*

Jews follow a lunar calendar, considerably older than the Gregorian calendar now commonly in use. If Joe Lieberman, an orthodox Jew and Democratic candidate for President of the United States, had won the nomination, you would have seen an abundance of t-shirts and bumper stickers advertising, "Lieberman in 5764."

9 781420 817027